AN ELE'
BIBL

UN

Finding Your Balance

Sandy Cooper

Copyright © 2017 by Sandy Cooper

Designer Book Template © 2017 Renee Fisher
https://www.reneefisher.com

Cover Design: Hannah Rose Creative http://hannahrosecreative.com
Cover Photo: Chris Montgomery http://chrismontgomery.ca
Author Photo: Rebekah Cooper

ISBN-13: 978-1974337309
ISBN-10: 1974337308

Dedication

To the Bible Study Babes:
Jennie, Jaime, Joy, Valerie, Susie, Laurie, and Linda.
Because of you, I had the courage to finally publish this.
You make Thursdays my favorite day of the week.

Table of Contents

Before You Begin...

I'm guessing you picked up this Bible study because you're feeling off-balance. You're probably feeling overwhelmed and unproductive. Maybe you can't quite figure out how to squeeze important people and duties into your already over-committed life. Perhaps what you "should" be doing and what you're actually doing are two different things. You're most likely looking around at other women and wondering how the heck they do what they do—and look so good doing it! Meanwhile you're running yourself ragged just to put a decent meal on the table and catch up on the laundry.

You probably don't even think you have the time to do this Bible study.

I get it. That was me through most of my 20s and 30s.

I felt constantly harried, overly busy, disorganized, and unfocused. Juggling my career, my home, my marriage, my ministries, and eventually my babies, left me feeling drained and inadequate. I desperately wanted balance, but balance felt impossible—at least for me. I remember looking at other women at work, at Target, in their cars passing by me, and I assumed they all knew something I didn't. I was convinced I was the only one who couldn't figure it out. I thought everyone had it together, but me.

This was the 90s. I couldn't Google "how to achieve balance" for answers. For half that decade I had stirrup pants and a spiral perm, but no Internet. (These were desperate times.) Yet, I was determined to crack the code. If a tip, a system, a secret ingredient to life-balance existed, I would uncover it.

So, I did what I always did when I wanted to figure something out in the 90s: I headed to Barnes and Noble and camped out in the self-help section. There I sat cross-legged on the floor with a giant, sugary, fat-free, caffeinated beverage, devouring book-after-book on time-management and home-organization.

Armed with my newfound information, I purchased a new day-planner (the obvious first step in time-management and home-organization prowess).

Then, I tweaked my laundry system.

And reorganized my closets.

And implemented a new diet and exercise regimen. (A small part of me has always believed I can fix everything by eating more green vegetables.)

And called my friends and ~~asked for advice~~ complained.

And vowed to be a better human.

And prayed—a lot.

But nothing worked—not even the prayer. Time with God was just one more thing I struggled to fit into my already-packed schedule.

There's no way anyone can actually do this balance thing. I may as well just succumb to my overwhelming, unfocused life. I give up.

After several desperate attempts and failures at achieving life-balance, I concluded balance was a myth, a unicorn—pretty and intriguing, but fake.

Then, in what I thought to be an unrelated act, I picked up a short Bible study written by Cynthia Heald called, *Becoming a Woman of Freedom*. At the time, I had no idea that the balance I was seeking was actually what the Bible calls "freedom." Freedom and balance are interchangeable terms. (The word "balance" also appears in the Bible, but only as it relates to scales or money. A Bible study about honest scales and bank accounts will not help you feel less frazzled, trust me.)

Heald's study helped me identify weights I carried—weights that, turned out, directly affected my on-going struggle with balance. Then it led me to Scriptures that specifically addressed those weights. As I applied these Biblical truths to my life, I began to feel lighter, freer. This gave me hope that maybe balance was possible, after all.

That year, I sat at my kitchen table with a toddler running around my legs and a baby in the bouncy seat next to me. I worked through that Bible study two more times. I highlighted and underlined and dog-eared the heck out of that little book. I was so inspired that I invited a group of young moms from my neighborhood into my messy house to study it with me. Later, I taught that same Bible study to a group of women at my church. Several of those women wanted to go through the study a second time, so I invited them into my home, and we went through it again.

In the process of teaching these truths to other women, I absorbed them deeply into my heart. Every time I taught it, God led me to more Scripture and more insight into the subject of freedom and life-balance—which, in turn, gave me more hope. I kept adding my new discoveries and personal illustrations to the Bible study material. Eventually, I had so much additional material, I realized I wasn't even teaching the Cynthia Heald study any longer. It grew into an entirely new study.

Not only that, but I also realized I was living the well-balanced life I had been striving for all those years.

Feeling like I may be on to something big, I wrote a 20-part blog series called, "Balancing God and Life." This series resonated so well with readers, that it became the basis for a new class I taught at my church called, "Balance That Works for Women." (Not the best title. It sounded like I was teaching on hormone health.) After creating the curriculum for that class, I realized I had enough material and life-experience to write on the subject of balance indefinitely. So, I ditched my old blog theme and launched an entirely new blog called, "The

Scoop on Balance," while also teaching the ever-growing material, yet again, to a group of women in my neighborhood clubhouse. (This is starting to read like my resume—sorry.)

In the winter of 2016, a small group of moms from my daughter's school gathered in my home on Thursday mornings to study (you guessed it) balance...*again*. And that group of precious women said, "*You need to publish this.*"

What you're about to read is the product of more than twenty years of learning, studying, writing, and teaching balance to women all over the world. Today, I invite you to be part of that ever-growing group of women who seek to live a life of balance.

I've never been more convinced than I am today: **Balance is a real thing**. It's neither a myth nor a unicorn. It's a worthy pursuit: tangible and entirely possible. I've seen it. I know real women who live well-balanced lives. I, Sandy Cooper, live a well-balanced life. And, at the risk of sounding like a late-night infomercial, I believe, in the very depths of my being, you can live a well-balanced life, too.

But wait, there's more!

Before you dive in, let me first tell you what balance is NOT:

- Balance is not doing everything.
- Balance is not doing everything your friends are doing.
- Balance is not doing everything your friends think *you* should be doing.
- Balance is not doing everything you see on Pinterest, Instagram, Facebook, or whatever social media venue is hip when you are reading this.
- Balance is not doing everything well.
- Balance is not doing everything by yourself, without help.
- Balance is not doing a little of everything each day.
- Balance is not spreading yourself equally among every person, task, responsibility, and expectation.
- Balance is not the absence of stress.

If you're pursuing any of the above things and calling it "balance," then let me break this to you gently: Balance, by any of those definitions, does not exist. Please do not pursue it. It's a recipe for failure and frustration.

Over the next 11 lessons, we're going to explore what real balance is and how we achieve it. In Part I, I will help you reconsider your current view of balance and reveal to you a workable definition based on Scripture and common sense. Then, together we will discover what God says about our time, our pursuits, and our attention.

In Part II, I will identify the barriers to balance—Perfectionism, The Comparison Trap, People Pleasing, and Busyness—and together we will learn practical steps to overcome them.

By the end of this study, you will feel more focused and less frazzled. You will have a clear understanding of Biblical balance and how to live it, today and forever. You will have hope that balance is not only real, but entirely possible. If you apply what you learn here, you *will* live a well-balanced life—I promise.

About this study:

If you are familiar with popular women's Bible studies, you may be used to seeing each lesson broken down into "weeks" and "days." I chose not to do that. I just call them "lessons." I want you to work at your own pace, whether it takes you a day, a week, or a month. Please spend as much time as you need on each lesson. Don't use your progression (or lack thereof) as another measuring stick against which you fall short. You can't "fall behind" in this study.

I'm working from the *New International Version* of the Bible for fill-in-the blanks. Whenever I reference another version, I will give you that Scripture.

hin each lesson, we dig deeply into scripture, but then I offer practical ways I apply the scriptural concepts to my life. We are all different, so my personal examples may not work for you. They are simply a catalyst for you to think of ways to apply these concepts to your life. Therefore, periodically, I invite you to consider your unique situation and make the lesson personal to you. Don't skip this part.

At the end of each lesson, I offer a Scripture-based prayer, using the Scriptures we studied in that lesson. Praying God's word is one of the best ways to get the Word into your heart. It also solidifies the lesson and helps you pray God's will over your life by declaring the Scriptures as truth over your circumstances. Of course, you can (and should!) pray to God as you wish. This is simply a launching pad and a template to get you started as you learn to pray God's word.

I'm so excited you're here. I know you are ready to get started, and so am I. So, let's do this.

Part I
Defining Balance

LESSON ONE

Priorities

"God, teach me what it means to forgo the riches of this life. Change me. I am spent."

Erin Loechner [1]

When I was growing up, my parents would pack all the kids into the station wagon and make an annual drive to an amusement park called Cedar Point. Like most amusement parks, Cedar Point had one section called, "Kiddy Land." (I'm not sure if that was its actual name or just the name my mom used.) Anyway, Kiddy Land had the typical rides for small children: a carousel, miniature bumper cars, and a half-dozen varieties of non-threatening rides, where the child sits on something (a car, a motorcycle, a boat) and goes around slowly in circles while pressing an annoying buzzer. Predictable, yet oddly enjoyable.

One ride resembled a big bowl with a disc in the middle of it. It was similar to the others—sit in the bowl and go in a slow circle on the rotating platform. What I didn't know was that, by putting your hands on the disk and turning it, you could also spin your big bowl. So, not only are you on a big rotating platform, you are also inside a spinning bowl *on* the rotating platform.

Being the youngest of seven kids, most of my early Cedar Point memories involve my older brothers and sisters going off to the roller coasters, while my mom and I hung out in Kiddy Land. Sometimes my mom stood at the railing, smiling and waving, like all good parents do.

Mostly though, she sat on a nearby bench, smoking a cigarette, while I ran freely from ride to ride (it was the 70s).

I remember one time when I was about 4-years-old, climbing into the big bowl, thinking it was just like all the other rides. As it started, I looked around at everyone smiling and laughing. I was smiling and laughing, too—at first. That was until some punk kid (now that I think of it, this may have been my brother), with very strong arms, started spinning my already-rotating bowl. The dual spinning action freaked me out. As any freaked out 4-year-old might do, I panicked. I wanted off! I wanted the stupid kid to stop spinning my bowl! I wanted my mommy! I kept trying to see her, but the spinning upon spinning made it impossible.

So, I did the worst possible thing: I got up on my knees and turned around backward in my seat. My intentions were good—I wanted to find my mom—but instead, this created a nauseating blur of spectators whizzing past me, lining the railing, and smoking cigarettes on the benches. I lost all sense of perspective and balance. I remember people on the ride yelling, *"Sit down! Turn around! Stop screaming! This is FUN!"*

No. No, this was not fun. Nothing could be less fun than this. My head was spinning, my vision was blurred, I wanted to vomit, and I couldn't find my mom. I screamed as loud as my little voice would scream. I just wanted off the ride. What was obviously fun for everyone else was terrifying to me.

I must have made quite a fuss, because the ride attendant stopped the ride so I could get off. I vividly remember stumbling off, head still spinning, stomach hurting, crying in my mom's arms. Kids were laughing at me. I was so embarrassed.

Stupid ride.

Spinny rides are a great metaphor for life and balance. For most of us, life is filled with routine events and rituals—eating, sleeping, working, playing. We finish one day and start it all again the next. It's good. We choose this on purpose. Mostly, these events are predictable, non-threatening, and quite enjoyable.

Sometimes, though, we hop on a ride that isn't quite what we had expected. What starts out as predictable and non-threatening is anything but that. Something is added to our life, and it's just too much. Things around us start spinning, and we can't quite figure out what's going on. We become increasingly overwhelmed, and we panic. *Stop the ride! I want off!*

Rather than sitting still and keeping our focus straight ahead, we desperately look around for something, someone, to give us relief. *Better time-management? A new Day-Timer? Essential oils? Less gluten?*

Good intentions, to be sure, but this only makes things worse.

Why does everyone else seem okay with this? Why am I the only one freaking out? What does everyone know that I don't?

Things get blurry. We lose focus. We lose perspective. We lose balance.

Balance. Everyone knows this term. Everyone uses this term. But everyone uses this term a little differently. So, first things first, let's take a look at some of the different ways people define balance.

Look up the word "balance" in a dictionary (on-line or an actual paper dictionary—do people still use actual paper dictionaries? I don't even know.) and write as many definitions as you can find:

_____

_____

_____

_____

_____

_____

You probably wrote words like, "even distribution of weight," "remain upright and steady," or "equal proportions." Maybe you found references to scales, money, art, sound, or wine. Perhaps even references to emotions.

Now, write what balance means to you. When you say you want balance in your life, what does that mean? What do you hope to achieve through this study?

_____

_____

_____

_____

_____

1. The Major Components of Long-Term Life-Balance

Roles

Sometimes, when I feel off-balance, what I really feel is, "*I just want to know what I'm supposed to be doing right now!*" In my most desperate times of imbalance, I had a thousand things to do, but didn't know *what* to prioritize or *how* to prioritize. No matter what I did, I felt like I was supposed to be doing something *else*. What confused me even more was looking around at what my peers were doing and comparing myself to them. (You mean, I need to do *that*, too?) This lack of "knowing" brought a sense of anxiety that I was continually missing God's will for my life and failing miserably.

As women, we inhabit numerous roles, each carrying a level of responsibility and commitment. Every role, responsibility, and commitment means more to juggle, more to prioritize. All this affects our balance. *Check all that apply to you:*

___I am a mother.
___I am a wife.
___I am a daughter.

__I am a sister.
__I am a neighbor.
__I am a friend.
__I am an employee/employer.
__I am a volunteer.
__I am a home-owner/tenant.
__I am a Christian.
__I am a _____.

Now, consider everything you do in a week related to those roles. Jot down a few of your regular (daily or weekly) tasks next to each role.

Look over everything you just checked and wrote. It's a lot, isn't it? You live a full life. No wonder you need balance.

Do you ever feel like you don't know what is most important? Do you ever feel like several high-priority people or responsibilities compete for your time and attention? Explain.

_____
_____
_____
_____
_____

Thoughts, Temperaments, and Beliefs

Sometimes when I say "*I need balance*" what I often mean is "*I need peace.*" Sometimes, I use balance and peace interchangeably. For me, levels of peace have little to do with my actual tasks and roles. **Levels of peace tend to flow directly from what I think and believe about my tasks and roles.** Some of these thoughts and beliefs are learned. Some are my hard-wiring, or my God-given temperament. *Here is a list of commonly-held beliefs that contribute to a loss of balance. Check all that apply to you:*

__I expect a lot of myself.
__God expects a lot from me.
__People expect a lot of me.
__I often feel overwhelmed.
__I am often overscheduled.
__I am undisciplined.
__I consider myself a perfectionist.
__Other women seem to "do life" better than me.
__I am often distracted (stupid phone!).
__I am afraid of failure.
__I am afraid of rejection.
__I am afraid of looking foolish.
__I am afraid of disappointing people.
__I am afraid of missing out.
__I don't have enough time to do what's important to me.
__I don't always know what to focus on.
__I don't get enough sleep.
__I don't get enough exercise.
__I don't spend enough time with God.
__Frustration and irritability are normal for me.
__I am an introvert (I recharge when I'm alone).
__I am an extrovert (I recharge when I'm with people)

Your roles and responsibilities, combined with how you think and what you believe, determine how you live. It's not just a full schedule (though that's part of it); it's also what you believe about yourself, others, and God that determines your level of balance.

I spent many years trying to prioritize the right things, but I was trapped under the oppression of People Pleasing, Perfectionism, and Busyness. There's nothing inherently wrong with having a full schedule, but it's never God's plan for you to be continually afraid, undisciplined, and overwhelmed. You can be striving to do all the right things, but if you're doing them out of fear or pride, you'll never live a well-balanced life. *Does this resonate with you? Explain.*

_____
_____
_____
_____
_____
_____

Distraction

The cruel irony is that being off balance keeps me focused on the fact that I'm off balance. Through most of my 30s, this preoccupation with balance (imbalance) was a major distraction in my walk with God. I was so depleted that I'm fairly certain I'd spent an entire decade asking myself the question, *"What is wrong with me?"* When all I thought about was how off-balance my life was, everything revolved around *my* needs, *my* time, *my* schedule, *my* rest—me, me, me! **How was I supposed to hear God's voice and do His will when all I could think about was myself?** This catapulted my balance issue beyond the physical and emotional realms into the spiritual realm.

Do you feel distracted by your lack of balance? How is it affecting your walk with God?

_____
_____

Balance: A Working Definition

Clearly, defining life-balance is complicated. What throws me off will not be the same thing that throws you off. It's not only our schedule, but it's also what we *think* about our schedule, about ourselves, and about God. We need to consider our temperaments, our strengths, and our weaknesses. We need to consider how all this affects our ability to hear God's voice.

So, after 20 years of struggling with/studying/achieving/teaching on balance, here is the best definition I can formulate, thus far:

Balance is a spiritual condition (peace), whereby I know my priorities (what I should do), and I live my priorities (how I should do it), through freedom in Christ (operating in my gifts and strengths, with right attitudes, and right thinking).

For the remainder of this study, when I say "balance," I mean that.

How would your life be different if you achieved this kind of balance?

_____

_____

_____

2. What Are My Priorities?

The Question

In your Bible, read Mark 12: 28-31 and Matthew 22:37-40
A teacher of the law asked Jesus a question. What was the question? (Mark 12:28)

_____

_____

_____

At the time this question was asked, the Jews had accumulated hundreds of laws—historians say as many as 613. Some Jewish leaders tried to distinguish between major laws and minor laws. Others thought all laws were equally binding and warned against drawing any distinction. So, asking Jesus which commandment was the "greatest" was controversial.

Isn't that like today?   As Christian women, we've accumulated a ridiculous amount of "laws" we need to prioritize—most of them not originating in Scripture. *This is what I must eat/not eat. This is how to properly keep a home. This is where I must shop. This is how to rightly discipline children. This is how often I must be intimate with my spouse. This is the correct way to manage finances. This is when/how/if I should pursue a career.*

While writing this lesson, my Facebook friends helped me identify these "laws" as they relate to parenting. I asked them to respond to the following statement: *"Good Moms (fill in the blank). I don't do that. Therefore, I am a Bad Mom."*

Here are the actual responses I received, along with a few of my own: Good Moms...

- Don't yell at their kids or lose it. Ever.
- Don't get easily frustrated or annoyed with their kids.
- Don't talk to their pet in a nicer manner than they do their children.
- Don't count the minutes till their kids are in bed or gone to school.
- Don't procrastinate on their kids' school projects.
- Don't feed their kids McDonald's.
- Don't order take-out Chinese for dinner, even when they've been at children's activities all evening.
- Don't overschedule the kids.
- Don't swear (in their heads or out loud).
- Don't need a glass of wine before helping with math homework.
- Don't have to wash paint off of the dog or scrape dried concrete off of the youngest baby's shoes.
- Never "check out" on the computer, but are always "checked in" to their children.
- Never consider watching an episode of *House Hunters* to be bonding time with a child.
- Never have to rely on other Mommy Friends to let them know what is happening at school.
- Never take away from family time to be with a friend.
- Never let their children stay on electronics all day.
- Never feel burdened or need a break from the children.
- Never sleep in.
- Are never too tired.
- Never express their needs.

- Never complain.
- Wake up early and stay up late.
- Do whatever it takes to keep the house clean, chores done, and exercise, so they can focus on mom business while kids are awake.
- Survive on very little sleep and are completely okay with that.
- Dive into any and every activity their child is involved in and have no selfish pursuits of their own.
- Have successful careers and show their children by example of how to be a contributing member of society.
- Volunteer at school.
- Stay home.
- Keep a spotlessly clean house.
- Are not bothered by a messy house.
- Keep up on laundry.
- Know how to let chores go so they can focus solely on their children.
- Make their own laundry detergent, baby food, and use cloth diapers.
- Keep a fully stocked pantry.
- Cook wholesome healthy, organic meals every night, which their children actually eat.
- Bake.
- Only serve dessert once a week, as a treat.
- Always do and say the right thing when it comes to discipline and never go too far or ignore it all together.
- Are always patient.
- Have chore charts and teach their kids how to cook meals and clean bathrooms.
- Do family devotions.
- Reuse milk cartons and egg crates to make crafts.
- Think paint and Play-Doh are awesome.
- Play with their kids—like really play, with Hot Wheels and Barbies. And they LIKE it.
- Are always up for something fun.
- Love having a house full of chaos.
- Are organized.
- Make every holiday, birthday, and vacation magical and

memorable.

- Take beautiful photos of "everyday fun" and post them on Facebook and Instagram.
- Are spontaneous.
- Homeschool.
- Teach their kids to read in preschool.
- Love helping with homework and never once utter the phrase, "I can't believe the stupid way they teach this!" or "Go away. I'm done."
- Bathe their kids on a regular schedule.
- Take their kids to church every Sunday.
- Organize regular play dates.
- Keep kids busy in activities that will enrich their lives.
- Keep up with all school papers and info that can only be found on the school's (poorly kept up) website.
- Stick to a healthy routine for wake-up, meals, school and nighttime.
- Enjoy spending every minute with their kids.
- Treasure and cherish their children all the time.
- Remember everything.
- Do it all with joy and gratitude. And good hair. (That one was mine.)

Sweet Baby Moses in a basket, what mother actually does all this? Never mind the sheer volume of qualifications for The Good Mom— did you notice how so many of these things are directly contradictory to one another?

A Good Mom has a career, volunteers at school, AND stays home?
Keeps a spotless house, BUT doesn't mind the mess?
Rarely sleeps, BUT is never tired?

What would you add to this list? Even if you aren't a mom, I'm sure you can relate. Change the word "mom" to "woman" and come up with your own list of laws.

———————————————————————
———————————————————————
———————————————————————

Until I started dissecting my balance issues, I had no idea how many subconscious expectations (laws) I'd placed on myself. I wasn't even sure which came from God and which came from me. I had a mile-long list of things I'd try to accomplish every day, and they'd all seem equally important. I desperately needed to know the most important thing.

Don't you sometimes just want to ask God: **"What is the most important thing, and I will do that"**? Just like the Israelites and their 600 laws, I want to know, plainly, where to place my focus.

The Answer

What did Jesus answer? (Mark 12:29-30 and Matthew 22:37-38)

———————————————————————
———————————————————————

When Jesus answered this question, he began by quoting the beginning of the Jewish confession of faith, known as the *Shema*. Since ancient times, devout Jews have been quoting the *Shema* every morning and every evening—so, both the teachers of the law, as well as the Jews listening to Jesus, were quite familiar with it. In other words, what Jesus said was nothing new.

Part I of the *Shema* is found in *Deuteronomy 6:4-9. Take a few minutes to read all of Deuteronomy 6, then write only verses 4-6 here:*

———————————————————————
———————————————————————
———————————————————————
———————————————————————

Loving God with all your heart, soul, mind, and strength is a lot more involved than what the brevity of the answer implies. Let's look at

Deuteronomy 6 a little closer to get more insight into the original context of The Greatest Commandment and make some practical applications for us today.

Fill in the blanks and answer the questions as you go. Remember, I'm quoting from the NIV.

Verse 4: "Hear, O Israel: The Lord our God, _____ _____ ___ _____."

This statement stood in radical opposition to all the religions of the ancient Near Eastern world. When Moses made this declaration, the Israelites were about to enter a land where their neighbors would worship countless idols and false gods. They'd be living among people who would think serving one God was crazy. Without a doubt, people would challenge them, ridicule them, and persecute them.

Today, people still worship many gods. We don't call them "gods," though. We call them "jobs," "political parties," "educational degrees," "houses/cars/clothing." Anything we elevate over God becomes our god—even our marriages, our kids, our passions, and our ministry efforts.

Our God, then, is not one. Our gods are many. Our love, devotion, and allegiance are divided among them. It's sad, but even within the Christian community, we consider it odd to be laser-focused on loving God the way Jesus had described.

I've been guilty of this. I've elevated my marriage and my kids above my relationship with God. Sometimes I place a higher value on my husband's opinion of me than I do God's opinion of me. That is idolatry. Jon makes a wonderful husband, but a terrible God.

When I'm feeling depleted or needy, I'm learning it's because I'm turning to people before I'm turning to God to have my needs met. This always leaves me feeling empty. Of course, we need people, but when we go to them instead of God or before God, we are in danger of idolizing them.

Can you think of anything you elevate over God? Have you ever thought of this as idolatry?

_____

_____

_____

Verse 6: "These commandments that I give you today are to be _____ _____ _____."

This does not mean the organ in your chest cavity, but rather the vital center of your being. The heart is where your emotions and sensibilities originate. So, when you impress something on your heart (in this case, God's law), it changes how you feel and think. It, quite literally, changes who you are.

Can you think of some practical ways to impress God's law on your heart?

_____

_____

_____

Verse 7a: "Impress them on your _____.

I don't know about you, but I have a lot of rules for my children that are not heaven/hell issues. *No texting at the dinner table. If you don't do your chores, you don't get allowance. Eat your vegetables before you get dessert.* Having such rules is not a bad thing. Some rules will not directly affect my child's walk with God, but they will help our household run more smoothly. These rules are usually my preferences, but have no basis in Scripture.

So lately, I've been challenging myself to live out Deuteronomy 6:7 by appealing to Scripture as I train and discipline my kids. When I explain a rule or boundary to my children, I ask myself if it has a basis in Scripture. If so, I explain the Scripture along with the rule or boundary. *You need to do your chores before you get paid because the Bible says if you are unwilling to work, you shouldn't eat (2 Thes. 3:10).* In this way, I'm impressing God's word on their hearts and showing them how to appeal to Scripture (not mom) as their final authority.

If you have children, think of a rule you've established in your home for them to follow. Do you know if this rule is based on a scriptural principle? If so, what is that scripture? Write that scripture below. Next time you implement the rule, try using the scripture with it.

Verse 7b: "Talk about them when you _____ at _____ and when you _____ along the _____. When you _____ _____ and when you _____ ___."

Since this command is in the context of speaking to your children, I do believe God literally wants us to work the word of God into conversations throughout the day with them. I thought I did a fairly good job at this, until I started listening to myself. Turns out, it's not the word of God I work into every conversation—it's nutrition. I talk about food and health all day with my kids. I remind them to eat. I explain why certain foods are good and lead to health and others are horrible and lead to sickness. I encourage them to make wise eating choices. All day. Every day. (My poor kids.)

That's nice. Good nutrition is important. But God wants me to talk about spiritual health with my kids. He wants me to remind them to consume the word of God. He wants me to explain why some choices are sound and lead to life and others are foolish and lead to death. He wants me to encourage them to make wise spiritual choices. All day. Every day.

While being concerned for their physical well-being and educating them on healthy choices is a good thing, my personal challenge is to be *more* concerned with what they put into their hearts and minds and to spend *more* time educating them on healthy spiritual choices.

When dealing with others—coworkers, friends, adult family members—this looks different. When your neighbor starts discussing music or politics or current events, you shouldn't interrupt with, "*Well, you know, the Bibles says…*" (If you do this, please stop it. People will find you annoying and tune you out, which is counter-productive to the purpose of this command.) Instead, speak lovingly. Speak truthfully. Speak kindly. Speak humbly. Speak patiently. Season your conversation with grace. When you open your mouth, find words that will build up and not tear down. This will sound exactly like God's law without ever quoting a single Bible verse.

Pay attention to what you talk about most throughout the day. If you are a parent, what do you say most to your kids? If it's not rooted in God's law, what is it?

_____

_____

_____

Verse 8: "Tie them as symbols on your _____ *and bind them on your* _____."

God wanted His people to have constant visual reminders of His laws—to keep them at their fingertips and close to their minds. God wanted everything they set their hands to do and everything they thought to flow from their love for God's law. The Jews eventually took this command literally, by placing pieces of scripture into small containers (called phylacteries) and strapping them to their arms and forehead.

Do you know what I tend to keep at my fingertips and before my eyes? My phone. I carry my phone around with me always—even from room to room in my house—and check it constantly—10 times an hour, at least! But my Bible? I keep that on the desk in my office. I read it once in the morning, and then I put it away.

I'm working on changing this. It's helpful for me to keep God's word in my line of vision. I write verses on sticky notes and index cards and hang them on my mirror or on my kitchen cabinet (in the place of honor…directly over my coffee pot). Sometimes, I leave my Bible open on the kitchen counter where I also charge my phone, so when I go there to check it, I will look at the Bible first. Sometimes, I place the Bible on top of my phone, so I'm forced to look at it first. When I'm not in a place where I can read the Bible, (like driving or doing housework), I try to listen to Scripture-based worship music.

Grab a sticky note or an index card and write Deuteronomy 6:4-6 on it. Place it somewhere you will see it several times a day. What are some other ways you can keep God's word in front of your eyes or at your fingertips?

_____

_____

_____

_____

Verse 9: "Write them on the _____ *of your* _____ *and on your* _____*."*

Because books were few and scattered, God commanded the Israelites to write the Law on their doorposts and gates of their homes. Like the previous command (vs. 8) some Jews took it literally, placing small boxes (called mezuzahs) with a piece of Scripture in them and attaching them to their doorposts.

In the same way, you can literally place scriptures on your doorframes and gates. That's very nice, but be careful not to miss the point: God's law should be the first thing people notice when they approach our homes. A framed piece of Scripture-based artwork hanging in the entryway is pretty. Yet how much more compelling it is when our home overflows with love, peace, grace, and hospitality. When people walk through our doors, do they see a household ruled by chaos and disorder or one ruled by joy and peace? Do they feel like an interruption to your busy day, or do they feel valued and heard? Are the relationships in your home marked by love and forgiveness or apathy and bitterness?

Imagine walking through the doors of your house as a guest. Describe what you see:

_____

_____

_____

Verse 12a: "be careful that you do not _____ _____ _____..."

When everything is going well, it's so easy to forget God, isn't it? We can so quickly absorb the mindset of the culture—that we are mostly responsible for our good fortune through our hard work and good choices—and forget that it is only by the grace of God that we have what we have. Everything good comes from God's hand.

Journaling helps me with this. The spiritual discipline of extracting the best parts from the previous day and thanking God for them has helped me see the hand of God in everything. If you're not a fan of journaling, no worries—you can still live with gratitude.

Can you think of a few other ways to keep God in the forefront of your mind?

_____

_____

_____

Verse 16a "Do not put the Lord your God to the _____..."

Because I've been around church most of my life, I sometimes find myself lulled into a familiarity with God that causes me to lose reverence for Him. I'm often lax in my commitments to Him and to my time with Him. I'm prone to question His power and His provision and blame Him when things go badly. In my worst moments, I've said, *"If you loved me, God, then you'd (fill in the blank)."*

Sometimes I see this behavior in my older children. Occasionally, my teens will approach me as if I'm their peer, not their parent. They will take a tone with me that clearly says, *"I think you're an idiot. If you really loved me, then you'd (fill in the blank)."* This is when I offer the firm warning that, while we share a close and loving relationship and they can come to me with anything, I'm not their buddy. I'm, first and foremost, The Mom.

(This is also when I utter the silent prayer, *Jesus, please let me stay alive long enough to watch my children have teens of their own. It would bring me so much joy. Thank you. Amen.*)

In the same way, I can approach God's throne freely and with confidence (Hebrews 4:16). I can ask questions and express my doubt. But this simple command about "testing" God reminds me Who's in charge. God is not my buddy. He doesn't have to prove Himself to me or to anyone. He is the Holy and Sovereign Lord, demanding my utmost reverence and respect. Loving Him with my whole heart, soul, mind, and strength means I also trust Him completely to act as He sees fit. And then, I obey.

Describe your approach to God. Is it casual? Formal? Comfortable? Reverent?

_____

_____

_____

In Deuteronomy chapter 6, God promises several things if we love Him and keep His commandments. *Read each verse and write the promise:*

Verse 2:

_____

_____

Verse 3:

_____

_____

Verse 19: _____
_____

Verse 25: _____
_____

Wow. All of that is what Jesus meant when He said, *"Love the Lord your God with all your heart and with all your soul and with all your mind."*

Now, in your Bible, look back at Mark 12:31 and Matthew 22:39. What did Jesus say is the second greatest commandment? Write it here:

_____
_____
_____

The Amplified Bible (AMP) renders His answer this way:

"The second is like it, 'You shall love your neighbor as yourself [that is, unselfishly seek the best or higher good for others]. (Matthew 22:39)

What a clear description of *"loving your neighbor"*!
Here, Jesus was quoting from *Leviticus 19:18*. What does it say?

"Do not seek _____ or bear a _____ against anyone among your people, but _____ your neighbor as _____."

Finally, Jesus made one last statement, and it's a big one. *Matthew 22:40,*
"_____ the Law and the Prophets _____ on_____
_____ _____."

He is simply saying, when we do these two things (love God with our hearts, souls, minds, and strength and love our neighbors as ourselves) we will—by default—keep all the other commandments, as well.

What does this mean for us? It means we do not need to worry about how we're going to keep all the rules or laws, biblical or not. Because if we love God and love others, it all falls into place.

So, back to the original question: What are our priorities? What is most important?

Answer: Love God. Love people.

That's it. Balance comes down to this: everything we do—every decision, every goal, every time-commitment, everything we say, everything we look at, everything we purchase—*everything*, must flow from loving God and loving others. When you do this, you will automatically be living a well-balanced life.

If all you get from this entire study is this—loving God and loving people—you will do just fine. (I mean, I want you to finish the rest of the study and everything, so don't stop here, for real.) This lays the foundation for everything else we'll study on balance. Remember it. We will refer back to it often.

And it's okay if you're still fuzzy on how to apply this information. In the remaining lessons, I will do my best to help you hear God through the Scriptures so He can show you how to love Him and love others.

We covered a lot of material in Lesson One, but don't worry, this is, by far, the longest lesson. *Before you move on, jot down your top three take-aways on the lines that follow. I'll ask you to do this at the end of every lesson. I want you to remember what you learned:*

1.

2.

3.

Let's pray:

Lord,

I come before You today, thankful that you have made my priorities clear. I will love You, Lord, with all my heart, with all my soul, with all my mind, and with all my strength. I will love my neighbor as myself. I will unselfishly seek the higher good for others. And from this love, everything else in my life will fall into place.

Lord, I will do everything you've commanded me to do, so that I, my children, and my grandchildren will always fear the Lord and enjoy a long life, and that all will go well with us and we will increase and prosper greatly. I will put your laws and commands in my heart. I will impress them on my children. I will talk about them when I am at home, and when we walk along the road, when we wake up and before we go to bed. I will keep your word continually before my eyes and be diligent to sow it into my heart. I pray that Your love and Your law be the first thing people notice about me. I pray that everything I set my hand to do and everything that comes out of my mouth flows from my love for You and for Your law.

Lord, when things go well for me, I will not forget you. I will always remember how you saved me and delivered me. I will give you glory for everything good in my life. I will not follow other gods. I will not put you to the test. As I walk, I will trust you to thrust out my enemies before me. For all of my days, Lord, You are my righteousness.

Thank you for clarity and focus and balance. In Jesus' name, I pray.

Amen.

LESSON TWO

Balance Basics

I've heard, read, and used many metaphors for balance. You probably have too. These metaphors can be harmful or helpful, depending on what they are, because they put a picture in our heads of what perfect balance is or should be. A metaphor will produce a clear mental image of what we are striving for and when we've achieved it (or not!).

For example, if you visualize balance as a "yoga pose," you may consider it failure when you lose your footing and fall over. Falling over in a yoga pose is bad. You can get hurt doing that. I've pulled muscles and twisted ankles holding yoga poses with improper form, and I promise you, it's not pretty.

(This is precisely why I choose to do yoga in my basement, privately, and not in a class.)

(Speaking of yoga class, what is up with "hot yoga"? Will someone please help me understand the allure? Is not the normal sweat-production of your body during exercise enough? Must you crank up the heat in the room and make it completely unbearable? Is torture the goal? Are you *hoping* to pass out?)

(Not that you asked, but I much prefer cool yoga. And fans. Lots and lots of fans. The cooler my yoga, the better.)

Maybe you visualize balance as a "balance beam." Falling off a balance beam is also bad. You can break bones or hit your head falling off a balance beam. Not only that, but chances are, if you are on a balance beam, you are performing before a panel of judges. Judges, well, *judge* you. They give you scores and deduct points if you stagger or stumble.

So, whether you are doing yoga in your basement or performing on a balance beam before judges, you are only a "success" when you strike the pose with precision and hold it with strength. Any wavering means you're doing it wrong.

If you visualize balance as a "juggling act" or "spinning plates" you may consider it failure when you drop something, set something down, or simply rest. If you drop plates, they shatter. If you drop balls, you have mayhem. Resting is out of the question—who can juggle or spin plates and rest at the same time? Jugglers and plate-spinners perform before an audience—they're purpose is to entertain. Thinking of balance in this way may cause you to believe—consciously or subconsciously—you cannot do anything halfway or let anything go, ever! If you do, you will let everyone down. You may feel like your inability to balance all the things all the time will cause, at the very least, disappointment, and at the very worst, irreparable damage.

Here's the thing: *no one* can navigate a balance beam perfectly forever, and *no one* can hold a yoga pose indefinitely, and *no one* can keep all the balls or plates in the air always. No wonder women conclude that balance is a myth! By those definitions, *it is!* This is why word pictures are so powerful—**you could be living a well-balanced life yet feel like a failure, simply because of the way you see balance in your mind.**

Before we go any further, let's do a quick review. If we want to achieve balance, we need to know what "balance" means. In Lesson One, we defined balance. *Look back at the definition of balance from Lesson One (page 22) and write it here:*

_____

_____

We all have a limited amount of energy and resources. Clearly, we can't do it all and be it all, all the time—or ever. We must learn to know our priorities and live them out. *What did Jesus tell us our first priority (the greatest commandment) should be?*

And the second?

That's right (you're so smart). It all begins with loving God and loving people. Everything else in a well-balanced life flows from that. Putting skin on that commandment can get tricky, though. How I live out "loving God and loving people" will look different from how you love God and love people. Don't worry, we'll figure it out. By the time we finish this study, we will have unpacked every part of that definition, looked at some very practical examples, and identified some major obstacles in our way.

In this lesson, we are jumping to the end of the definition of balance and discussing "right attitudes and right thinking." With "knowing your priorities" set firmly as the first layer of the foundation, the second layer is this: **having proper perspective about your priorities**. In other words, balance is not only a byproduct of what we do, but also *how we think* about what we do!

In your Bible, read the following scriptures. How does each verse address the importance of viewing circumstances from the proper perspective (God's perspective)?

Genesis 50:20

Isaiah 55:8-9
_____

_____

Romans 8:28
_____

_____

Colossians 1:9-12
_____

_____

From these verses, we see that how we view our circumstances, whether from God's perspective or ours, has everything to do with our levels of joy and peace (and remember, peace = balance). Our perspective also directly impacts our effectiveness in whatever roles we currently hold. After studying balance for almost two decades, I have identified four helpful ways to think about balance. Each of these reframes our actions so we view them from God's perspective. I call them Balance Basics. In this lesson, we'll discuss the first two.

Balance Basic #1: Balance is Measured and Achieved Over the Course of Time, Not Day-to-Day

The Toddler Diet

When my daughter, Rebekah, was a toddler, she was a picky eater. (Which I realize now is the very definition of being a toddler.) But back then, as a new mom, it freaked me out. (Which I realize now is the very definition of being a new mom.)

Every once in a blue moon, she'd eat three square meals and two healthy snacks. She'd clean her plate and ask for seconds on her veggies. Those were really good days. Most days, however, were a hodge-podge of eating confusion. In the morning, she would devour her well-balanced breakfast of bananas and peanut butter on whole-wheat toast. Then by noon, she wouldn't touch her lunch.

At 4:00 p.m. she'd be hungry and beg for Goldfish and apple juice.

Then she'd only eat cubed chicken for dinner.

The next day, she'd decide she no longer liked bananas for breakfast.

The following day? She'd be all, *"ONLY BANANAS, YOU FOOL! And never chicken, ever again. I will not eat it here or there. I will not eat it anywhere!"*

The day after that, she'd refuse anything but dry Cheerios, a slice of American cheese, and the remnants of petrified mystery food from under the kitchen table.

The following day: all broccoli, all the time.

Since Rebekah was tiny for her age and inconsistent in her eating, I concluded in my new-mom brain that she was malnourished—and I, of course, was a failure.

Then I spoke to her pediatrician, who, first, confirmed that I was insane. Kidding. She was compassionate and empathetic and assured me I was a doing a great job. Rebekah was well-nourished and growing, but I wasn't so sure. That's when she recommended I stop looking at her nutrition each individual day. Instead she said, *"Look at what she eats over an entire week, and I think you'll feel better."*

When I did that, I discovered that, while Rebekah was, indeed, a picky eater, she was actually a very healthy—and yes, *well-balanced*—eater. What I formerly saw as daily fluctuations and inconsistencies, evened themselves out completely over a week's time.

Nothing changed in Rebekah's diet, except my view of it.

Stepping back and broadening my perspective from "daily" to "weekly" changed everything and brought me peace.

I used to view life-balance the way I viewed Rebekah's eating habits.

On the days I carved out time for bible study, prayer, exercise, housework, chatting with friends, volunteering, creating magical memories for my children, personal development, cooking dinner from scratch, and having sex with my husband, I was balanced.

On the other 364 days of the year, I was a failure.

Did you know it's impossible to cram everything meaningful into a 24-hour period, every single day? (Hello, unicorn!)

When I stepped back to get a broader view of my life, I saw it differently. Not much changed in my actual schedule, but broadening *my view* of my schedule from daily to weekly (or monthly, annually, seasonally) brought peace and freedom.

I realize now, some days God calls me to spend several hours studying the Word and to turn off my phone notifications. When I do this, I may not interact with any humans for an eight-hour stretch—that's me today, as I write this.

Other days, it's all humans, all day long, as I volunteer at school, meet a friend for coffee, stand in the driveway to talk to the neighbors, and help kids with homework—that was me yesterday.

Some days, I hold a feverish child, watch a Disney Channel marathon, and order pizza for dinner.

Other days, the kids are at school, and I scrub the house from top to bottom, while laundry runs through the washer and dryer, and a home-cooked meal simmers in the crock-pot.

Some days, I spend all day in the car, carting children from activity to activity.

Other days, I quietly and privately stay home and make my way through my to-do list.

Some days Jon comes home late, I go to bed early, and we only communicate over text.

Other days, we hang out all morning, go on a date at night, and talk until our throats hurt.

If I look at these days individually, each is off balance. However, if I look at them together, over the course of a week? A month? *A life?* Just like Toddler-Rebekah, the off-balance days, strung back-to-back-to-back, comprise a well-balanced life.

Rate yourself: "I tend to view balance as something that must be achieved perfectly each day."

This is not me   *This is sometimes me*   *This is totally me*

1   2   3   4   5   6   7   8   9   10

Scales vs. Pendulum

For years, I visualized balance as a scale—the kind of scale where each side has to be the exact same weight or it's lopsided. Just like the illustration of Rebekah's diet, I saw balance as something I needed to adjust perfectly every day. One extra task or responsibility on one side of the scale meant a task or responsibility of equal effort and time had to go *off the scale*, lest the extra thing would cause the scale to tip and throw off the entire day! I was constantly manipulating each day down to the minute to achieve what I perceived to be balance. Parenting, cooking, cleaning, exercising, praying, socializing, ministering, resting, wife-ing—every day, I was constructing and reconstructing the tasks to squeeze it all in. (Note: I was trying to do this with babies and toddlers in the home. This, my friend, is a recipe for crazy.)

In real life, my days and my children cannot be manipulated down to the minute. In real life, balance does not look anything like scales. In real life, balance looks more extreme, like a pendulum.

For example, I've had school situations arise with my children where I've spent an exorbitant amount of time talking with a kid, making phone calls and lunch dates with trusted friends for advice, and holding meetings with the principal and teachers. When that happens, it encompasses my whole week and sucks up all the time I would normally spend on writing, exercise, and house-keeping.

Other weeks, we have had back-to-back social situations—family in town, parties, evening school events—and I've had no time to be alone, run errands, or read.

Sometimes because of Jon's work schedule, he and I barely see each other for days at a time, except a quick hello and goodbye at morning and night.

Each of these individual days looks extreme—and they are. However, when I anticipate these extremes, and I *lean into them* instead of fight them, each extreme becomes part of a well-balanced life.

In fact, it's the very movement from one extreme to the other that gives life its energy. Just like a clock, it's the pendulum's movement, back and forth, back and forth, that keeps the clock running. If you interrupt the flow of the pendulum, the clock stops.

I've learned, instead of trying like crazy to fit everything on the scale *just-so*, every day, perfectly balanced, I hop on the pendulum and ride it over. Then, when my days or weeks swing into one extreme, I can make deliberate changes in my life to swing it back into the opposite extreme, instead of stressing out, trying to fit it perfectly into each day, every day.

This gives my life rhythm and energy and keeps it running.

What does that look like in real life? This is how I might purposely swing the pendulum from one direction to another:

In Social Interaction: If I have a day or two of constant conversations or meetings, I take a day or two to recharge in seclusion. That means I stay home, turn off my phone notifications and get off social media. (This is the introvert in me. You may need to recharge in social situations. Do what you need to do to get your balance.)

In Working: When writing has taken a back seat to everything else, as it often does, I will block out a whole day to crank out some new material.

In Parenting: If Jon and I have a week or two where we feel like we are doing nothing but disciplining and correcting the kids, we may take a fun road trip or do something recreational to break the tension, laugh, and remind them that we are not complete monsters.

In Marriage: Since Jon has a demanding job, requiring full days, late nights, and early mornings, we balance it with quiet weekends and regular date nights. After an exhausting season of parenting, where teens had been the focus of our lives, we shifted to a much-needed focus on our marriage relationship.

In Finances: If we have a season of extreme expenses, we will go on a buying freeze for a month to rebuild our savings account.

In Eating: If, in one week, I attend a party, plus several dinners out, plus frozen pizza on a school night, I will balance it out the next week with ultra-clean eating. Maybe, I'll even incorporate a 24-hour fast in there. In fact, after the two-month holiday season, I always take the entire month of January to get my healthy eating back on track. Periods of feasting followed by periods of fasting.

In House Work: As much as I try to do just a little every day, the children outnumber me, and it eventually gets out of hand. I need to balance the accumulating filth with a whole cleaning day, where I go room-by-room and whip the house back into shape.

When I can, I am proactive and *schedule* my extremes. For example, I may look at the calendar and see a string of back-to-back busy days coming up, so I purposely schedule low-key days on either end to counterbalance the busy ones.

Pendulum-Balance.

Back and forth. Back and forth.

One extreme and then the other.

Rhythm and energy.

Rate Yourself: "*I tend to see balance as a scale—move one thing on and take another off to stay perfectly balanced.*"

This is not me   *This is sometimes me*   *This is totally me*

1   *2*   *3*   *4*   *5*   *6*   *7*   *8*   *9*   *10*

This is a good place to mention that living a well-balanced life requires constant flexibility and adjustment, too. We can't find a good rhythm and flow and then expect to stay in that forever. This can be difficult for people like me, who thrive on routine and ritual. We need to be very intentional about remembering that balance looks different depending on our situation and season.

Balance as a single woman with a full-time job is different from balance as a married woman with a full-time job. Balance as a stay-at-home mom to babies and toddlers is different from balance as a work-from-home mom of teens and a tween. **From season to season, circumstances and priorities change. What works in one season, will not necessarily work for the next—in fact, it usually doesn't.** And you will have hundreds of mini-seasons within those major seasons, where we need to stay connected to God in order to receive wisdom—*His wisdom*—to prioritize for that unique season.

Read the following scriptures from the Amplified Bible and answer the questions related to seeking God for wisdom in the affairs of everyday life.

Proverbs 16:3 (AMP)

3 Roll your works upon the Lord [commit and trust them wholly to Him; He will cause your thoughts to become agreeable to His will, and] so shall your plans be established and succeed.

What happens to your thoughts when you roll your works upon the Lord?

_____

_____

_____

What happens to your plans?

_____

_____

_____

Proverbs 4:25-26 (AMP)

25 Let your eyes look right on [with fixed purpose], and let your gaze be straight before you. 26 Consider well the path of your feet, and let all your ways be established and ordered aright.

As you walk with God, which direction should you be looking? Describe what that might look like on a practical level? What should you be doing before you take a step (vs. 26)?

_____

_____

_____

Proverbs 24:3-5, 13-14 (AMP)

3 Through skillful and godly Wisdom is a house (a life, a home, a family) built, and by understanding it is established [on a sound and good foundation], 4 And by knowledge shall its chambers [of every area] be filled with all precious and pleasant riches. 5 A wise man is strong and is better than a strong man, and a man of knowledge increases and strengthens his power...13 My son, eat honey, because it is good, and the drippings of the honeycomb are sweet to your taste.14 So shall you know skillful and godly Wisdom to be thus to your life; if you find it, then shall there be a future and a reward, and your hope and expectation shall not be cut off.

What are the three things upon which your house should be built (vv. 3-4)?

_____

_____

_____

What are the benefits of allowing Wisdom to be the foundation of your life?

_____

_____

_____

Balance Basic #2: Balance is Measured and Achieved by Seeking and Obeying God, Not Anything or Anyone Else

One of my favorite scenes in the Disney Classic, *Mary Poppins*, is when Mary Poppins meets Jane and Michael Banks for the first time. Mary Poppins mesmerizes the children with an array of antics as she pulls large objects—one-by-one—out of her magical carpetbag. After digging to the very bottom, she finds the last item: a tape measure. When the children ask, "*What's that for?*" She replies, "*To see how you two measure up.*"

First, she measures little Michael from head to toe. Rather than giving her a number, the tape measure reads, "*Extremely stubborn and suspicious.*" Next, she measures Jane. Hers reads, "*Rather inclined to giggle. Doesn't put things away.*"

Finally, Mary Poppins measures herself. Hers reads, "*Mary Poppins. Practically perfect in every way.*"

In addition to word pictures and metaphors, we also use all kinds of measuring tapes and measuring sticks to determine our levels of balance. We measure our balance against performance reviews at work, USDA recommendations of fruit and vegetable servings, the number of friends (real and virtual) in our tribe, staged and filtered photos on Pinterest and Instagram, the number on the scale, the bank statement, the cleanliness of our floors, and let's not forget the Good Mom List from Lesson One.

While they vary greatly from woman to woman, I've found these measuring sticks basically fall into three categories: Productivity, Comparison, and The Opinions of Others. I'll mention them briefly here, but will discuss each one in depth in later lessons.

Productivity: Because we live in a society that idolizes busyness, we often measure ourselves against an exhausting standard. If we are not working, striving, and producing from the time we wake up until our heads hit the pillow at night, we are failing. The more we accomplish in the day, the better. This leaves no room for rest, for creativity, for recreation, for prayer—all elements of a well-balanced life. Productivity is a nice goal—I love productive days—but it's a horrible measuring stick for balance. (We will dive deeply into productivity and how it relates to Busyness in Lessons Ten and Eleven.)

Comparison: We look around at women who appear to be doing everything and doing it well. We don't measure up, of course, because it's all an illusion—no one is doing everything and doing it well. Then, we heap shame upon ourselves for not measuring up to something that doesn't even exist. I have never met a woman who does not struggle with comparison on some level. It is nothing but a trap. (We will dive deeply into Comparison in Lessons Six and Seven.)

Opinions of Others: Sometimes how other people view our day, our season, or our life can mess with us, just as much as (or more than!) our own thoughts can mess with us. We may be confidently pursuing our "extreme," knowing full-well that the pendulum will swing back eventually. While others, who only get a snapshot view of our life, see us as unbalanced and are all-too-willing to let us know. We then second-guess our choices, our decisions, and our priorities. What people think about our choices overrides our priorities. Receiving wise counsel is important (I highly recommend it), but not at the expense of what you know God has told you to do—that's called People Pleasing. (We dive deeply into People Pleasing in Lessons Eight and Nine.)

When we measure ourselves against anything but obedience to the Word of God and God's specific direction for us, we get into trouble. God can and will lead us into some crazy extremes. Sometimes what God calls "balance" looks like anything but! The last thing we need is some faulty measuring stick telling us we are doing it wrong.

Nothing illustrates this better than bringing home a new baby. Those first few weeks are just stupid. You're sleep-deprived and un-showered. You're strapping another human to your chest and staying home for days at a time. You're napping mid-day (if you're lucky) and up at 2:00 a.m., 4:00 a.m., 6:00 a.m. You take maternity leave. You are the beneficiary of a meal train. (I love the meal train—please bring me dinner.) You're scaling enormous laundry piles. You're sporting engorged and leaky breasts. Poop and puke are everywhere.

A new baby turns every conventional idea of balance on its head. And yet, this is exactly how God designed it to be. So, in the midst of this ridiculousness, you still have perfect balance.

I lived a version of this life for about a three-year period, first with the birth of my son, followed by his death at nine months of age, and then the birth of my daughter nine months later. From the time my son was born, until my daughter was about 18-months-old, I pulled back on almost everything outside of my home (and many things inside my home) to focus on holding my babies, moving through my grief, and rebuilding my faith. I spent most of my time alone or with my husband. I never hired a baby sitter. I didn't work outside the home for most of that time.

By all conventional standards, my productivity levels were at an all-time low. I remember sitting in the rocking chair holding babies, looking out the nursery window, seeing all my female neighbors driving away with styled hair and full make-up every morning. Meanwhile I was in a ponytail and stirrup pants. My house was a wreck. My flowerbeds were overgrown. My dinners consisted mostly of take-out and canned soup—seriously, for a full three years.

From an outsider's point of view, I needed to move on—put on some mascara, get a part-time job, dust my mantle—*something!*

But God knew what I needed—healing, mostly. It's hard to concentrate on healing when you're worried about your dusty mantle. What a tragedy it would have been had I measured my balance against the working mom down the street. I couldn't know this at the time, but I only had nine short months with my son. I can't imagine if I had wasted that time fretting about flowerbeds! Given the chance to do it again, I wouldn't change one single choice from that three-year period. (Well, the stirrup pants, maybe.) That time of extreme pulling back was foundational to the parent, wife, and woman of God I am today.

Granted, most people do understand the need to pull back after a birth or a death (or, in my case, both). You may have seasons, though, where God draws you into something deeply internal, that no one understands—not even you.

A few years ago, God led me to set down all outside commitments— good and godly commitments, where I was operating in my gifts and helping people—and I didn't understand why. I fought it a little. (Okay, I fought it a lot.) I loved what I was doing. I had goals and aspirations for writing and speaking. My kids were in school. I had the time. I couldn't understand the inner feeling that God wanted me to pull back instead of move forward. Not long after that, the reason became crystal clear when one of my kids entered a time of personal crisis. I needed to be 100% available to that child. Had I been obligated to writing contracts and speaking engagements, I would not have been here. This crisis lasted almost three years. I had no idea what was coming, but God did. I'm so thankful I didn't plow through and strive for some outward standard of balance.

Maybe God is not asking you to set things down or pull back. Maybe instead, He is leading you to take on more than seems logical. Maybe He's calling you to focus on that creative project and add that to your already-full schedule. Or maybe He's leading you to something unsafe and life-altering: the mission field, inner city ministry, or serving the underprivileged in some way that doesn't appear practical or logical. Maybe He's calling your family to adopt or foster a child. Or perhaps take on a second job or plunge all your savings into starting a business. This is the time you must neglect all the world's measuring sticks and pursue God's mission.

He may not tell you this side of eternity why you need to neglect one thing for a season and focus on another. It all seems unbalanced, but it's not. It's perfectly imbalanced-balance. It's part of a bigger picture that we will see clearly, later.

The key to balance is not to strive for constant equilibrium. The key to balance is not to pursue what everyone else is pursuing. The key to balance is not even to look inside yourself and follow your own heart.

The key to balance is to cling to God, realizing only He knows what our days and weeks hold. Only He can poke and prod us toward balance—whatever that means for our season or our day. Listen intently to the voice of God concerning your season and your priorities for that season. It may just feel like a nudge or a pause. You may have a "yuck" feeling about moving forward in one direction and a peace about moving in a different direction. Whatever you do, obey what God says.

Read the following scriptures below. Use the prompts to reflect how seeking God and obeying Him leads to balance.

Psalm 10:4a
"In his pride the wicked man does not seek him;"

In my life, I find it's my pride that keeps me from seeking God. It's the belief that I can handle the situation in my own strength and skill. In your life, how do you rely on your strength instead of seeking God?

_____
_____
_____

Psalm 10:4b
"in all his thoughts there is no room for God."

My brain is always full. At any given time, I feel like a computer with twenty open windows. When my brain is cluttered, I have a terrible time focusing on God. How cluttered is your mind? Can you take some practical steps to allow some space for God in your thoughts?

_____
_____
_____

Hosea 10:12-13
"12 Sow righteousness for yourselves, reap the fruit of unfailing love, and break up your unplowed ground; for it is time to seek the Lord until he comes and showers his righteousness on you. 13 But you have planted wickedness, you have reaped evil, you have eaten the fruit of deception. Because you have depended on your own strength and on your many warriors…"

Here again, God draws a correlation between wickedness and depending on your own strength. How can depending on your own strength lead to evil or deception in your life?

_____
_____
_____

Psalm 105:3-4
"3 Glory in his holy name; let the hearts of those who seek the LORD rejoice. 4 Look to the LORD and his strength; seek his face always."

Have you noticed the first signs of feeling off-balance are a lack of joy and a lack of strength to accomplish what you need to do? What do these verses suggest you do when that happens?

_____
_____
_____

Tucked in the book of Isaiah is one of my favorite chapters in the entire Bible. In it, God, speaking through the prophet, contrasts a life of one seeking God the wrong way with one seeking God the right way. As we seek God's will and direction for our lives, doing it the right way is vital. The benefits of a life bound to the will of God greatly exceed anything we can create on our own. Perfect balance is found in complete submission to His will and His ways.

In your bible, read Isaiah 58, and then meet me back here to answer the following questions.

Verse 1 says, "Declare to my people their rebellion..." What is their rebellion, exactly? (vv. 2-4)

_____
_____
_____

When I read this in light of women and balance, I see the woman who does all the right "Christiany" things: maybe she goes to church and serves on the hospitality team; she probably attends weekly Bible study; she teaches her kids to pray before meals; she declares her devotion to God; she promises to follow Him.

But then she's irritable with her husband, and she snaps at her kids. She's always stressed, and she blames God for heaping too much on her plate. Instead of praise, she complains to her friends, (she calls it venting.) Instead of following God, she does what she feels like (she calls it vegging).

Then, she cries to God saying, *"I'm fasting, I'm praying, I'm doing all this stuff for You, Lord, and You aren't answering my prayers!"*

Sometimes, I am this woman. Maybe you are this woman, too. God calls this behavior "rebellion." Ouch. This portion of scripture underscores the importance of, not only seeking Him, but also doing what God says. (Not just a form of what He says, not just kinda what He says, but exactly what He says.)

Have you been this woman? Explain.

_____

_____

_____

Read verses 7 and 10: What are some things God tells us specifically to do?

_____

_____

_____

Read verse 13: What does God tell us to do here? How does this buck the current culture of busyness and productivity?

_____

_____

_____

Read verses 11-12: What are all the benefits of obeying the Lord listed here?

_____

_____

_____

When we obey the Lord, what are the names we will be called?

_____

_____

_____

As I write this lesson, it's summer. I'm sitting on my front porch, overlooking our flowerbeds. The daylilies, cone flowers, and hydrangeas are in full bloom. Every few minutes, I see butterflies hover over them. I hear crickets and locusts. Sometimes, I see a humming bird. Our garden is teeming with life.

This is the image of the well-balanced woman we see in Isaiah 58. This is how our Heavenly Father describes us when we seek Him and obey Him: Refreshing, thriving, bearing fruit, restoring, repairing…

Doesn't that sound like real life? Not real life, as in the life you are actually living, but the real life you were meant to live? What a contrast to running in circles, without purpose or direction, stressed, and overwhelmed.

This week, as you consider "right attitudes and right thinking," may you humbly seek God and His will for your day. This is where you begin. Balance flows from that.

Before you move on to Lesson Three, write a few things you want to remember about this lesson:

1. _____

2. _____

3. _____

Let's pray:

Jesus,

Your Word says as the heavens are higher than the earth, so are Your ways higher than my ways and Your thoughts higher than my thoughts. And we know that in all things You are working for my good. Help me to see my life and my circumstances from Your perspective.

I ask You to fill me with the knowledge of Your will through all wisdom and understanding that the Spirit gives, that I may live a life worthy of You. I desire to please You in every way: bearing fruit in every good work, growing in the knowledge of God, being strengthened with all power according to Your glorious might, so that I may have great endurance and patience. I will give joyful thanks to the Father, Who has qualified me to share in the inheritance of His holy people of light.

I will let my eyes look right on, with fixed purpose, and let my gaze be straight before me. I will consider well the path of my feet, and let all my ways be established and ordered aright. Through skillful and godly wisdom is a house (a life, a home, a family) built, and by understanding it is established [on a sound and good foundation]. By knowledge shall its chambers [of every area] be filled with all precious and pleasant riches. Please give me skillful and godly wisdom.

I will seek You and Your strength. I will seek Your face always. I will make room for You in my thoughts. I will sow righteousness for myself and reap the fruit of unfailing love. Shower your righteousness on me.

God, I ask that through me, You would loose the chains of injustice, untie the cords of the yoke and set the oppressed free. Show me opportunities to share food with the hungry, provide shelter for the poor, and clothes for the naked. Then my light will break forth like the dawn, and my healing will quickly appear. My righteousness will go before me and the glory of the Lord will be my rear guard.

When I call, You will answer. When I cry for help, You will say, "Hear am I." My light will rise in the darkness and my night will become like the noonday. You will guide me always. You will satisfy my needs in a sun-scorched land and strengthen my frame. You will make me like a well-watered garden, like a spring whose waters never fail. Through you and in You, I will repair and restore the broken. When I honor you, when I rest in You, I will find my joy in the Lord. You will cause me to ride in triumph on the heights of the land and feast on Your inheritance.

In Jesus' name.

Amen.

LESSON THREE

Balance, Basics, Continued

"I've learned that you can't have everything and do everything at the same time."

Oprah Winfrey

Balance Basic #3: Balancing Life Requires an Eternal Perspective

When I was a new mom, I had a hard time knowing what to focus on. Depending on what I read or to whom I spoke, it seemed like everything was important: what I fed the baby, how I fed the baby, how I dressed the baby, where the baby slept, how long the baby was held, the toys I bought, the car seat I chose, the pediatrician we saw. I also subscribed to several parenting magazines. (The Internet wasn't a thing yet.) So every month, I had ten new things to add to my "must have for baby" list.

I was so confused.

That's why it was (and still is) helpful for me to talk to experienced moms with grown kids. They offer a unique perspective, telling me *"this matters"* and *"this doesn't matter."* Or *"you won't remember this"* and *"I've done it both ways, and it turned out fine either way."* This helps me prioritize and put my mind at ease.

Even now as I write this, having two high-school students helps me prioritize better for my elementary student to prepare her for high school. I know, for example, not to stress out about the "family tree project" and instead focus on math facts and reading!
Hindsight gives clarity and direction.

Isn't that why we love reading deathbed speeches? Don't you just relish every word of the person who is at the end of life and declares, "*I spent a lot of time worrying about* _____, *but now I see, what really matters is* _____"?

Wouldn't it be helpful to have someone like that coach us on a daily basis? Someone who sees life from eternity's perspective to tell us what *really* matters and what doesn't?

Enter Jesus.

He sees life from the position of eternity. He looks at how we spend our time, our energy, our money, our focus and can tell us *"this matters"* and *"this doesn't."*

In your Bible read Matthew 6:19-20, 25-34. The chart below is a summary of what Jesus said.

<u>*Do Not Worry About or Focus on This*</u>
1. Treasures on this earth
2. Money
3. Your life
4. What you will eat
5. What you will drink
6. Your body
7. What you will wear
8. Tomorrow

<u>*Instead, Seek This*</u>
1. Treasures in heaven
2. God
3. The kingdom of God
4. God's righteousness

But how? How is it possible to live in a finite, tangible world, where we must work and eat and dress and build, yet focus on the infinite, intangible world that we cannot see or touch?

The key is to look for the eternal value in the midst of everyday life.

I learned to do this best when we were building our house. Choosing to build a house was my husband's dream. I confess to you right here and now, I was not entirely on board. With all of Matthew chapter six swirling around in my mind, I had to ask God to show me the eternal value in spending an entire year and a ridiculous amount of money on something that could be destroyed in a moment.

He answered that prayer on Toilet Selection Day. Yes, toilets had their very own special day, and I was dreading it. By this time in the building process, I was beyond overwhelmed. I had no bandwidth left to select toilets.

As the sales clerk explained the various features and options of every toilet on the showroom floor, I began to glaze over. Who knew toilets came with so many options? I couldn't believe I was wasting my afternoon obsessing over where our poop was going to go. Literally.
I mentally asked God to help me find the eternal value in toilet selections. And He did. It wasn't in the toilet itself, but in the sales clerk helping me. Suddenly this wasn't merely a sales transaction, it was an opportunity to see and talk with a human being.

I started joking with her about toilets. Then, I asked her a few questions about her family. (I reasoned that she was becoming quite familiar with my family's excretory habits, so why not?) It wasn't long before she started opening up to me about her personal life. I learned she was going through a divorce and was about to launch her child to college—big, sad changes. I hugged her right there in the toilet showroom and offered to pray for her. By the end of that encounter, I had selected my toilets *and* sought the kingdom of God.

Toilets are temporary. Sales clerks are eternal.

Anyone who has built a house knows that choosing toilets is one of the hundreds, yay, thousands, of selections to be made. Right now, I'm sitting in my house looking around at cabinets and walls and flooring and paint colors. Each one is a story of a hundred "temporary" decisions. And the trim-work! Holy cow, the trim-work in our home is so intricate and beautiful—and, also temporary.

Jesus tells me not to worry about it, though. It could all burn up in a fire tonight. Trim work may not be eternal. But do you know what is? The guy who built it. His name is Park. Every day while we were building the house, I'd picked up my kids from school and drive to the new construction to see the progress Park was making on the trim. We also went to see Park. As Park chiseled and shaped our mantle, bookshelves, crown molding, and wainscoting into existence, I'd talk and joke with Park, and we'd all marvel at his artistry.

One day, Park asked if he could show me pictures of items he built for his kids. Then he showed me pictures of his kids. That day, I drove away from our new home praying for Park and his kids.

Trim is temporary. Park and his kids are eternal.

As the weeks turned into months, and I was spending all my free time (and most of my not-free time!) building our new home and packing up my old one, I asked God again to help me find eternal value in all of it. God answered that prayer by giving me a glimpse into the finished product. Not the decorated, painted, furnished version, though. He showed me the eternal stuff: my children growing up in the house, seeking God in the quiet of their bedrooms, entertaining friends in our basement and around our kitchen table. He showed me friends and family visiting on the porch over a cup of coffee. He showed me how I'd be opening my home to women teaching this very Bible study; how I'd sit here in these rooms and write words that would reach women around the world, as I'm doing this very moment.

Houses are temporary. My kids are eternal. Their friends are eternal. My family and friends are eternal. My Thursday morning Bible study ladies are eternal. You are eternal.

John Ortberg in his book, *When the Game is Over It All Goes Back in the Box²*, suggests that we go through a little exercise to remind us where to store our treasures.

Imagine you have a pad of sticky notes. Now, write "temporary" on each one. Then go around your home and place them on all your stuff that has no eternal value. Put one on the car, on the house, on the countertops, and the carpet. Place one on the checkbook and the debit card. Place one on each item of clothing and each pair of shoes. (I know you love those cute ones, but, girl, they are temporary.) One on the computer. One on the treadmill. One on the washer and dryer. One on the iPhone.

Then take another pad of imaginary sticky notes and write "forever" on each one. This time, place one on your spouse, on your children, on your boss, on your mother-in-law. Place one on each of your friends. On the barista serving up your latte and the greeter at Wal-Mart. Place one on your next-door neighbor. Your child's teacher. The guy who just cut you off in traffic. The client that sucks the life out of you. The person you dislike most in the world. (Which, incidentally, may be the client who sucks the life out of you.)

Can you imagine how differently we'd behave if everything with temporary and eternal value was labeled as such? Can you see how just recognizing the difference between the two would bring so much balance?

When I consider how much of my life is spent just maintaining our stuff—cleaning our stuff, fixing our stuff, organizing our stuff, replacing our stuff, eating our stuff, stuffing more stuff into our already-stuffed drawers and closets—it makes my heart hurt. So often, when I'm thrown off balance, it's because of this: too much time spent on the temporary.

Why is it we seem to build our lives around what is temporary and squeeze in time for what is eternal?

Why do we spend hours and hours maintaining all our stuff yet complain that we have no time to feed our souls? Why do we waste hours scrolling through Facebook and Instagram, but claim we cannot find time to consistently cook a dinner and sit at the table with our family? How can we show up every week to watch *The Bachelor,* but find it such a chore to make it upstairs before bedtime and pray with the kids?

Read this next statement carefully. Then underline it.

Wise and balanced people build their lives around what is eternal and squeeze in time for the temporary, not the other way around.[3]

Francis Chan says, *"Even now, I am working to make sure that my family is set up for the future. When most people make that statement, they are talking about financial security for their last few years on earth. When I say it, I'm referring to the millions of years that come after that. People accuse me of going overboard in preparing for my first ten million years in eternity. In my opinion, people go overboard in worrying about their last ten years on earth."*[4]

I still wrestle with this, even after God so clearly showed me eternal value the year we built the house. So last year, I began taking small risks with my time to sow more intentionally into the eternal: *What if I got up 15 min or 30 min earlier so I can pray longer? What if after I drop off the kids at school, I spent an hour in worship instead of immediately tackling my to-do list? What if I start teaching a Bible study each week? What if I lead our church's women's ministry?*

What originally felt like "risks" ended up being wise investments. As a result, I have more clarity, more direction, more focus, and more balance than I ever have had.

Even now, I hear God gently nudge my heart. He's saying, "*Don't waste today. Invest your resources wisely—your time, your money, your energy. I didn't give all this to you so you could waste it. I gave to you for an eternal purpose. Sow it there. Live richly toward God. And when you do this, balance will flow naturally from it.*"

Prayerfully consider some practical ways you can begin looking for eternal value in your material life. List them here:

_____

_____

_____

Balance Basic #4: Balance requires knowing my gifts and protecting my limitations.

When I was a little girl, I was told I could do anything I set my mind to do. As a teen and emerging adult, I believed my options were endless and my possibilities, infinite. Society fed me and my female peers a steady diet of "women can do it all and have it all." Commercials sang, "*I can bring home the bacon, fry it up in the pan, and never ever let you forget you're a man.*" (I can work, cook, AND have great sex!) Television portrayed smart, successful career-women, who were also loving mothers with impeccable homes and incredible fashion sense. (I miss you, Claire Huxtable.) So throughout my 20s and 30s, my peers and I pursued education, career, relationships, and motherhood. We believed we were invincible.

Somewhere in those two or three decades of adulthood, a subtle shift occurred. **No longer did I believe I *could* do anything; instead, I felt the pressure that I *must* do everything.** Most women I know still feel this pressure on a daily basis.

I've often wondered, did my mother feel this pressure? Did my grandmother?

Probably not.

In the U.S., this cultural pressure on women to do everything is a recent phenomenon. From colonial times until the 1940s, most Americans believed a woman's natural environment was her home and family. During wartime, however, society was interrupted. The men were off fighting in the war, so women had to enter the work force to keep the country running. Government propaganda during World War II was responsible for much of the change in society's acceptance of women in the workplace. Posters, radio programs, magazine articles, and advertisements showed women in overalls with greasy hands for the first time. These changes enabled women to enter factories by the millions and proved that women were capable of much more than having babies and washing dishes. This was a good change.

However, it wasn't long before obvious problems arose. Childcare, housework, and transportation were all left up to the working woman. Childcare was, by far, the biggest issue, because profit-making childcare centers did not exist. Housework was an all-day task. (There were no washers, dryers, or automatic dish washers, and everyone cooked meals from scratch.) Still, women were expected to handle all these tasks, plus work outside the home, by themselves.[5]

Fast forward to today.

The pressure to do it all is stronger than ever before. We don't see posters of women in overalls and greasy hands—instead, we see glossy ads of sexy business executives in pencil skirts and stilettos, *holding a baby*. Now, not only must I do everything, but I must do everything *at the exact same time*.

On top of all that pressure, we hear a steady, incessant whisper: *"Not only CAN you do and be everything you want to do and be, you deserve to do everything. Look at Pinterest and Instagram and Facebook...see all the people doing and being everything? Everyone else is doing it. You must do it, too. DO EVERYTHING!"*

This not-so-subtle societal pressure keeps nearly every woman I know in a constant state of striving. No matter what we do, it's never enough. The insatiable spirit of discontentment drives women to exhaustion.

Remember reading the "Good Mom" list in Lesson One? Describe how you felt as you read it the first time.

As Christians, we take it one step further. We add a spiritual element and quote the Bible. In the midst of striving for more, exhausted, and depleted, we declare, "*I can do all things through Christ who gives me strength.*" *Phil 4:13*

I have a problem with this.

Not with women working outside the home or pursuing education, necessarily. I'm so thankful for the women who have gone before me to fight for my rights as a woman in this country. I have a college degree and have every intention of providing the same for my daughters. I want equal rights, equal pay, and equal opportunities for women.

And not necessarily with those who pursue career and motherhood simultaneously. Every circumstance is different, and I firmly believe women should prayerfully make the choices that are best for themselves and their own families.

My problem is with the Christian community—you and me—succumbing to and adding to the societal pressure already heaped on women. I don't think scripture tells us we are invincible or that we can do everything. In fact, I think it says something quite different—maybe even, the opposite.

We have weaknesses. We have limitations. I believe weaknesses and limitations are as much a part of our intricate design as our strengths and gifts. God gives us weaknesses and limitations, strengths and gifts—all of it—on purpose, *for His purpose*. We dive more deeply into strengths and gifts in Lesson Seven. Today, we will explore weaknesses and limitations, and we will begin by looking at Philippians 4:13 in context.

In your Bible read Philippians 4:10-13

Paul wrote this letter in 61 A.D. to the church in Philippi, while he was in a Roman prison. He had previously established a church there, and they had sent him a financial gift. The purpose of the letter was to thank them for the gift and encourage them in their faith.

Look closely at verses 11-12. What is it Paul is saying he has the ability to do with God's strength?

_____

_____

_____

After all Paul's experience with various circumstances in life—being in need or having plenty, well-fed or hungry, living with much or very little—he expresses his firm confidence that nothing would be required of him that he would not be able to perform. God's strength would provide him with contentment in any and every circumstance.

Read the last sentence again, and circle the word "contentment."

"I can do all things" is better translated, "I have strength for all things." It's not a literal "all things," as in each and every thing that Paul decided to do. Rather, "all things" refers to the duty and suffering chosen not by Paul himself, *but by the Lord*.[6]

So, Paul is not saying he can do all things nor is he saying, "*I can do anything I decide to do.*" His declaration is not an encouragement for us to strive for more and more.

This is what Paul is actually saying (paraphrased):

"Thank you for sending me money, but even if you did not send money—even if I was hungry and in need—I'd still be okay. I have learned the secret to contentment: It is resting in the strength Christ gives me to endure whatever He calls me to."

Now, read this passage in The Living Bible:

10 How grateful I am and how I praise the Lord that you are helping me again. I know you have always been anxious to send what you could, but for a while you didn't have the chance. 11 Not that I was ever in need, for I have learned how to get along happily whether I have much or little. 12 I know how to live on almost nothing or with everything. I have learned the secret of contentment in every situation, whether it be a full stomach or hunger, plenty or want; 13 for I can do everything God asks me to with the help of Christ who gives me the strength and power.

I don't know about you, but I've been guilty of misunderstanding and misusing this scripture. I have been the one at the point of utter exhaustion, chasing whatever society told me I "deserve," and quoting, *"I can do all things through Christ who gives me strength!"* However, Paul is saying something quite different. Instead of Paul encouraging us to go get more, he's telling us to be content with what we have!

Ladies, let's not look to society for our lessons on balance or achievement or fulfillment. We cannot allow society to dictate our limits and boundaries. Society has no regard for limits and boundaries. Society says, *"You can do it all; you can have it all, and you can look fantastic while you're doing it."*

That's a lie.

One thing I know is this: I am not invincible and neither are you. I have weaknesses and so do you. This is not an insult. This, my friend, is freedom.

I used to hate my weaknesses and limits. I felt like they got in the way of what I wanted to do, so I'd get very frustrated with myself. I thought that God hated my weaknesses, too, because they got in the way of what God wanted me to do. I felt like I had to either apologize to God and to others for having weaknesses, or hide them altogether!

If I did identify a weakness or a flaw in my character (which was often), I thought God was revealing it to me so He could fix me. I thought God wanted me to continue working on all my weaknesses, so eventually I wouldn't have weaknesses any longer. I thought this was the definition of becoming more like Christ.

(Actually, it's the definition of discontentment, exhaustion, and insanity.)

I was so relieved to discover my warped view of myself and my weaknesses did not match God's view of me and my weaknesses.

Read 2 Corinthians 12:7-10 below:

7 "Therefore, in order to <u>keep me from becoming conceited</u>, I was given a thorn in my flesh, a messenger of Satan, to torment me.

8 <u>Three times I pleaded with the Lord</u> to take it away from me.

9 But he said to me, "<u>My grace</u> is sufficient for you, for <u>my power</u> is made perfect in weakness." **Therefore I will boast all the more gladly about my weaknesses, so that <u>Christ's power</u> may rest on me.**

10 That is why, for Christ's sake, I delight in weaknesses, in insults, in hardships, in persecutions, in difficulties. For when I am weak, then <u>I am strong</u>." (bolding and underlining mine)

Turns out, human weakness is not something God hates. Instead, human weakness provides the perfect opportunity for God to descend upon us and to show us His strength.

Look at verse 9. The phrase *"may rest upon me"* can also be translated *"may come down upon and dwell within me"* or *"may spread a tabernacle over me."* Isn't that beautiful? The Apostle Paul wanted to give the readers of this letter this magnificent image of the Shekinah glory of God—the dwelling or settling of the divine presence of God on the earth—descending upon us when we are weak.

Weakness is not an invitation for God's correction or chastisement. Instead, it attracts His glory and His power.

Nothing illustrates this better than Christ on the cross. When the Lord was at His absolute weakest, He displayed His greatest power.

In your Bible, read 2 Corinthians 13:4, and write it here.

_____

_____

_____

So, what does all this mean for you and me?

While you cannot do everything, you can do anything God has called you to do. If He called you, He will equip you, even when it's hard. The key is asking God what He wants you to do, and then finding your strength in Christ to do it.

What hard thing is God calling you to do right now? How can you find your contentment and strength in Him as you do it?

_____

_____

_____

Knowing and understanding your weaknesses is just as vital as knowing and understanding your gifts. Weaknesses take various forms. Understanding which is which can help you know how to address them.

Weakness as a Character Trait: I'm mostly an introvert. I like being with people, but I work best alone where my days are quiet with lots of margin, and when they consist of a slow, steady pace. Also, I'm highly sensitive to everything—good or bad. I feel everything deeply. Therefore, I get overwhelmed rather easily. Too much stress causes me to crumble. (It's so fun living with me.)

These weaknesses or limitations are most apparent when I compare myself to my extroverted, fast-paced, low-emotion husband. (He's like a freaking machine.) For years, I beat myself up because keeping up with him was sometimes hard for me. I often felt like I was holding him back, literally and figuratively. When I wanted to settle in, he was ready to take flight. My slower pace coupled with my ultra-sensitivity sometimes makes it difficult to be a loving wife, because I become overwhelmed when he's just getting started. These things get in the way of what I want to do or what others expect of me.

Likewise, sometimes my need for slow and steady days with margin built in makes it difficult to be an effective and loving parent. If you have children, you know that, no matter how well you plan, the pace of your day is often completely out of your control.

I've tried repeatedly to change these things about myself, but I can't. No matter how hard I try, I don't like busy, face-paced days. This is simply my hard-wiring.

Since I cannot change these things about my character, I need Christ's power to rest on me so I can be the wife and mother my family needs me to be. God can give me energy when I feel like I can't keep up. He can give me patience and flexibility when days are chaotic. He can help me extend grace and mercy when my feelings are hurt, and yet he doesn't take away the weakness or limitation. He gives me power to thrive within them, in spite of them.

"Will I choose to be a victim of my circumstances, using my differences and difficulties as excuses for why I failed to do great things? Or will I decide to view my differences as superpowers that can enable me to live better and live out a story worth telling?"
Nathan Clarkson [7]

Rather than hate my weaknesses, I've learned to appreciate them—love them, even. Those weaknesses that make me ultra-sensitive or cause me to lag behind my fast-paced husband are the exact traits I need to thrive in other areas of my life. My love for being alone, my love for order and routine, my ability to feel all things deeply—all these traits are what I draw upon most when I write. Each of those character traits/weaknesses was lovingly placed in me by the hand of God to use for a specific purpose.

What character traits do you have that make it difficult to be effective in your God-given roles?

_____

_____

_____

How are those same weaknesses an asset to other God-given roles?

_____

_____

_____

Weakness as a Vulnerability to Sin. When I do become overwhelmed or stressed (my hard-wiring), I'm tempted to lose patience with my husband and children. I snap at them. I'm sarcastic. I say and do hurtful things. This is not a character trait, but outright sin. I must be aware of this weakness so I can protect myself from getting overwhelmed or stressed in the first place. If I do find myself where I'm stressed and overwhelmed, God can strengthen me so I have the power to choose love over sin. So even when our weakness is a temptation or vulnerability to sin, the power of God resting on us gives us the ability to resist the temptation.

Look up Romans 6:22 in your Bible. Write it here, word for word.

_____

_____

_____

God wants you free from sin. Ultimately, you can overcome this type of weakness completely if you continue to live a life submitted to God.

What sins are you most vulnerable to? Is it gossip? Pride? Bitterness? Gluttony? (Hint: if you aren't sure, think about the sins you commit over and over, or the ones you slip into when you are hungry/angry/lonely/tired.) List them here.

_____

_____

_____

How do these sins prohibit you from thriving in your God-given calling?

_____

_____

_____

Whether your weaknesses are hard-wiring or vulnerability to sin (or both!), it's important to identify them and be aware of them. Your weaknesses or difficulties were either divinely placed by God or they were put there by the Enemy (see 2 Corinthians 12:7). But take heart! Either way, God will use them for His purpose. Either way, your weaknesses are a perfect environment for God's power to rest upon you. In fact, Paul goes so far as to say he boasts about his weaknesses! That's a far cry from hating them.

Look back at the underlined phrases in 2 Corinthians 12:7-10. Identify five specific ways God can use weakness for His purpose:

Verse 7:

_____

_____

Verse 8:

_____

Verse 9:

_____

_____

Verse 9: (look for another one in this verse)

_____

_____

Verse 10:

_____

_____

One way we can approach and address our weaknesses and limitations is by setting up healthy boundaries to protect them. *What? Protect them? Don't we want to get rid of them?* Not necessarily. Remember, our weaknesses are prime real estate for Christ's power to take up residence. The only weakness we should actively try to eliminate is sin. The character traits—attributes and tendencies divinely placed there by your Loving Creator—those, we want to protect. They are in you for a reason.

Just like you might put a brace on your weak knee before you exercise, setting up a boundary around your weakness helps give added support so you don't "injure" yourself or others. This approach of protecting my limitations and weaknesses has been one of the most refreshing, liberating, and well-balanced things I have ever done for me and my family.

What does that look like? Well, basically it means I put some boundaries in place to protect my limits and keep me from wanting to scratch everyone's eyes out. The following are some practical examples of these boundaries. Yours will look different, depending on what you are trying to protect.

- My husband and I do regular date nights. This protects me from feeling overly sensitive if he needs to work late or when a child needs his attention over mine.

- I discipline myself to go to bed early and rise at least an hour before everyone in my household. This gives me uninterrupted quiet time to seek God alone every day and protects my family from having to interact with Tired Sandy. (Lately, my machine-like husband has been getting up the same time as me. What the heck? You guys, I just can't handle human interaction at 5:15 a.m.)

- I carve out at least five hours a week to exercise. This protects my sanity.

- I try to stick to a To-Don't List—not to be confused with a To Do List. I say "no" a lot—especially to people who want me to help with committees, oversee functions, or attend social outings. These are things I'm quite capable of doing (and may even enjoy), but prayerfully set aside for the sake of balance. This protects my calendar so I don't unintentionally overcommit my time and eat up my margin.

- I try to observe a Sabbath once a week, usually on Saturday. I take a break from all my normal work—I don't cook, don't clean, or do a single load of laundry. I sleep in. I relax. I read. I recreate. I enjoy my family. This also protects my margin and helps me recharge. (We'll talk a little more about Sabbath in Lesson Eleven.)

- I practice solitude. I intentionally find time every single day where I am completely alone and quiet—no phone, no computer, no music, no talking. My children are in school and also old enough to stay home alone, so I am able find solitude on a regular basis. However, when my children were little, I had a regular babysitter. I used her often, so I could have quiet built in to my week. (Money well-spent, by the way.) This protects my mind so I can hear God speak to me.

When I neglect these boundaries, I get overwhelmed and "off balance." This is when I lose my temper. I become jealous of my friends, suspicious of my husband, and impatient with my children. It isn't long before I spiral down further. I get anxious. I question my calling. I doubt my purpose. This is a big red warning light that I must intervene. If I don't, I run the risk of falling into a period of clinical depression.

(I'm always surprised how feeling overwhelmed can so quickly spiral out of control!) For me, protecting my weaknesses and limitations is no joke. It is the added support I need so I don't become vulnerable to sin and sickness.

I know this particular list of boundaries isn't for everyone. Maybe you are a social person who loves being busy and active, and you become depleted when you've been alone for too long. My husband, my daughter, and some of my closest friends are like that. If that's you, you need to protect your social time with friends and family as fiercely as I protect my quiet time.

Now it's your turn. Look up at your list of character traits you identified as weaknesses. What boundaries can you begin putting into place to protect those?

_____

_____

_____

_____

What about your specific vulnerabilities to sin—how can you put some boundaries in place that help you avoid those situations in the first place?

_____

_____

_____

I'm confident that, as you find eternal value in the ordinary moments of your life and submit your weaknesses to God, you will begin to live out your priorities in the freedom, peace, and power God intended for you. As we are learning, this is true balance, after all.

Before you go, don't forget, to jot down three things you don't want to forget from this lesson:

1. _____

2. _____

3. _____

Let's pray:

Dear Lord,

Today I ask that you please help me to find eternal value in my every day, ordinary life. Help me refrain from storing up treasures on earth, where moths and vermin destroy, and where thieves break in and steal. But, instead, store up for myself treasures in heaven. Wherever my treasure is, there my heart will be also.

I will not worry about my life, what I will eat or drink, or about my body, what I will wear. The birds do not reap or sow and yet You feed them. The flowers do not labor or spin, and yet, Solomon in all his splendor was not dressed as beautifully as them. If this is how you feed the birds and clothe the flowers, I can trust you to feed and clothe me. I will walk in faith. I will not worry, because You are my Heavenly Father, and you already know what I need. I cannot add a single hour to my life by worrying.

Jesus, please help me learn to be content in every circumstance, whether in need or in plenty, whether well-fed or hungry. Free me from the pressure to do everything and be everything. I can only do and be what You ask of me. I can do all things through Christ who gives me strength.

Lord, you created me and you know me intimately. You know my every strength and every weakness. Your grace is sufficient to overcome all my weaknesses, for Your power is made perfect in weakness. Therefore, I will boast all the more gladly about my weakness so that Christ's power will rest on me. That is why, for Christ's sake, I delight in weaknesses, in insults, in hardships, in persecutions, in difficulties. For when I am weak, then I am strong.

In Jesus' name.

Amen.

Part II
Barriers to Balance

LESSON FOUR

Perfectionism

"Perfectionism is slow death...If everything were to turn out just as I would want it, just as I would plan, I would never experience anything new. My life would be an endless repetition of stale successes. When I make a mistake, I experience something unexpected."

Hugh Prather [8]

It was October 2, 1993. Our giant wedding was over, and our friends and family were helping us transport carloads of wedding gifts from the reception hall to our new house. With about 340 guests at our reception, we'd received a lot of gifts. Add to those the gifts that had been mailed to our house prior to the wedding, plus the gifts we'd received from three bridal showers, and that equals... um...*a lot of gifts.*

It was getting late, and we still had a two-hour drive ahead of us to the hotel. We needed to hurry so we could enjoy our wedding night *blush* before catching an early morning flight to the U.S. Virgin Islands for our honeymoon. In our haste, we directed our people to ~~neatly place~~ quickly dump the gifts in the dining room alongside the others, and off we went to begin our life of wedded bliss.

Upon our return home, the mountain of boxes and white ribbon greeted us at the front door. We couldn't miss it, because it flowed out of the dining room and into the entryway, blocking the walkway from the living room to the kitchen.

I pushed the pile against the wall, allowing us access to the kitchen, and decided I'd wait to open and sort the gifts when I had more time.

See, I was waiting for the perfect day.

A day when I could open each gift, one-at-a-time, preferably with my new husband at my side. I wanted to slowly and thoughtfully read through each and every card, remember each person who bought us a gift, write a proper, heart-felt thank you note, and then find the ideal place for the gift in our new home.

Unless of course, it was a duplicate gift, at which point, I intended to place it in a separate pile with the attached receipt so I could return it or exchange it for something more suitable.

And I wanted to do it all in one day, from beginning to end. I wanted to do it *perfectly*.

Those were the days of a demanding 50-hour-a-week job, endless volunteer and church responsibilities, and–oh yeah–*a new marriage*. Jon and I barely had enough time to dine together once or twice a week, let alone find a day with enough hours strung together to complete the task the way I wanted it done (*perfectly!*). So, the gifts remained in a giant pile against the wall in our dining room.

For days.

For weeks.

For months.

Every once in a while, my groom would stroll over to the gifts and open one up, at which point I would become completely unglued *for-fear-the-card-would-become-detached-from-the-gift-and-I-would-never-know-who-sent-it-and-I-wouldn't-be-able-to-send-a-thank-you-and-I-wouldn't-be-able-to-organize-it-the-way-I-wanted-to*...*GASP* *DON'T TOUCH THE GIFTS!!!! I WILL DO IT WHEN I CAN SIT DOWN AND DO IT PERFECTLY!!!* (I said this a lot those first few months.)

By February (four months later!), Jon had had enough. He was sick of walking through our front door to be greeted by a mountain. He was sick of side-stepping presents every time he headed to the kitchen. He was sick of me procrastinating on this long-overdue task.

That's precisely when he took matters into his own hands. One day while I was not home, he moved all the gifts from the dining room into the basement. He opened most of them in transit, disposing of wrapping paper and envelopes at random. He separated cards and receipts from the gifts and tossed them into a pile in the corner. He took out a few of the more useful kitchen gadgets and put them away in cupboards and drawers. The rest of the opened gifts, he piled on the floor in an unused portion of our basement.

Then he went about his day as if he had done nothing wrong.

I was devastated. Paralyzed.

He was forcing me to deal with the mountain of wedding gifts, yet I had no idea how to address it if I could not do it perfectly and completely, from start to finish. I honestly did not know how to do *anything*, if I could not do it perfectly and completely from start to finish.

Hello, my name is Sandy Cooper, and I am a Recovering Perfectionist.

I used to wear the badge of "Perfectionist Sandy" proudly. In my first real job interview (just a few years before the Wedding-Gift-Fiasco), I had stated "perfectionism" as one of my strengths. I thought it was a good thing. It meant to me, at the time, that I was thorough and paid attention to detail. Had my perfectionism been only that, it would have been a great asset, indeed. Even today, in some scenarios, Perfectionist Sandy is quite useful. Like when I need to organize a closet, or edit a manuscript, or sanitize a toilet. Detailed and thorough work is vital in those situations. In the other 95% of my life, however, it's downright oppressive.

In addition to paralyzing me at the thought of any giant project, Perfectionist Sandy is not at all helpful when she's dealing with children. She's a terrible marriage counselor. She seriously messes with my self-esteem. She taunts me while I attempt to move through my daily list of household chores, plan and/or enjoy a family vacation, try to publish a blog post, or write a Bible study lesson—even *this* Bible lesson on Perfectionism. Ugh.

In a word, perfectionism is a huge barrier to my balance.

Perfectionism and Balance

Remember the Balance Basics we covered in Lessons Two and Three? Perfectionism outright defies each one of them:

- **Balance Basic #1: Balance is Measured and Achieved Over the Course of Time, Not Day-to-Day**. A perfectionist craves order in every area. She cannot see "chaos" or "messy" as part of an overall well-balanced life. A perfectionist holds every situation, every day, and relationship against an impossible standard. Rather than flexibility and adjustment, a perfectionist can become very rigid and fearful. If she finds a method or schedule that works, she is afraid to deviate from it. Rather than seeing the big picture, she focuses on the detail.

- **Balance Basic #2: Balance is Measured and Achieved by Seeking and Obeying God, Not Anything or Anyone Else.** A perfectionist measures balance by what others expect of her, either expressed or imagined. In fact, a Christian perfectionist usually believes that God requires perfection from her—which flies in the face of grace and the work accomplished on the cross.

- **Balance Basic #3: Balancing Life Requires an Eternal**

Perspective. A perfectionist has a hard time determining what is eternally relevant and what is not. Everything feels relevant.

- **Balance Basic #4: Balance requires knowing my gifts and protecting my limitations.** A perfectionist is usually painfully aware of her limitations, but not in a good way. Instead of setting healthy boundaries to protect her from exhaustion, distraction, or over-commitment, she uses her limitations as a club with which to beat herself because she can never measure up to the standards she has set.

What is Perfectionism?

Gordon Flett, professor of psychology at York University in Toronto, has been studying perfectionism for decades and is an expert in the field. He defines it this way:

"Perfectionism is the need to be - or to appear - perfect. Perfectionists are persistent, detailed, and organized high achievers. They vary in their behaviors; some strive to conceal their imperfections, others attempt to project an image of perfection. But all have in common extremely high standards for themselves or for others. Perfectionism is not officially recognized as a psychiatric disorder. However extreme forms of perfectionism should be considered an illness similar to narcissism, obsessive compulsiveness, dependent-personality disorder and other personality disorders because of their links to distress and dysfunction." [9]

This definition, though not intended by Flett to be spiritual, points toward spiritual truths:

1. *"Perfectionism is the need to be - or to appear – perfect…some strive to conceal their imperfections, others attempt to project an image of perfection."* Whenever you conceal something or project something that is not there, you are living in deception. Deception and all forms of lying originate with Satan, the Father of Lies. (See John 8:44)

2. *"They vary in their behaviors…"* This fact recognizes the truth that

not all perfectionists are alike or manifest their perfectionism in the same way. God created us as unique and distinct individuals. (See Ephesians 2:10)

3. *However extreme forms of perfectionism should be considered an illness…because of their links to distress and dysfunction."* Perfectionism is a spiritual weight that contradicts the freedom promised to us in the Word of God. (See Galatians 5:1)

Many people get overwhelmed with detail or procrastinate from time to time, but not all people are perfectionists. Perfectionists display specific behavior patterns that characterize them as such. Look at this list of perfectionist traits[10] and circle the word indicating how well each one describes you on a typical day.

1. You cannot stop thinking about a mistake that you made.

not at all   sometimes   absolutely

2. You are intensely competitive and cannot stand doing worse than others.

not at all   sometimes   absolutely

3. You either want to do something 'just right' or not at all.

not at all   sometimes   absolutely

4. You demand perfection from other people.

not at all   sometimes   absolutely

5. You will not ask for help, if asking can be perceived as a flaw or weakness.

not at all   sometimes   absolutely

6. You will persist at a task long after others have quit.

not at all   sometimes   absolutely

7. You are a fault-finder who must correct other people when they are wrong.

not at all   sometimes   absolutely

8. You are highly aware of other people's demands and expectations.

not at all   sometimes   absolutely

9. You are very self-conscious about making mistakes in front of others.

not at all   sometimes   absolutely

Dr. Flett and his colleague Dr. Paul Hewitt are the masterminds behind *The Multidimensional Perfectionism Scale*, a tool intended for use by psychologists to help their clients understand their perfectionist behavior and how it relates to mental and physical health problems, relationship problems, and achievement difficulties.[11]

The questionnaire identifies three types of perfectionists. *Circle the one(s) that describe you:*

1. Self-oriented perfectionists expect perfection of themselves.

2. Other-oriented perfectionists demand perfection from others.

3. Socially-prescribed perfectionists think others expect perfection from them.

Perfectionists reveal themselves in three distinct ways. *Check the one(s) that describe you:*

_____1. A self-promotion style that involves attempts to impress others by bragging or showing off. This type is easy to spot in others, as they often irritate other people.

_____2. Shunning situations in which they might display their imperfection. This is common even among young children.

_____3. A tendency to keep problems to oneself and can include an inability to admit failure to others.

Pulling together the information thus far, I would describe myself as a combo self-oriented/socially prescribed perfectionist who has a tendency to keep problems to myself so I don't bother people.

I am highly aware of other people's expectations of me—or at least what I perceive their expectations to be. Sometimes these people are the real people in my life—my husband, my children, my friends, my extended family. Having two teens has resurrected a lot of perfectionist tendencies in me, because teens are notorious for noticing and naming every single imperfection in a parent. Other times, I have what I call "a committee of accusers" in my head, telling me to do better and try harder (more on this in a bit).

What about you? How would you describe your perfectionist style?

_____

_____

_____

_____

If not you, then do you recognize someone you love in those descriptions? Maybe a spouse, a child, a friend, or a sibling? (If you do not struggle with perfectionism but love someone who does, I highly encourage you to work through this lesson in order to understand them better and point them in the direction of freedom.)

The Root of Perfectionism

My favorite game as a child was *Perfection®*. (Of course, it was.) The object of the game is to fit all the little geometric pieces in their proper place before the time runs out. If you don't, the whole game explodes and the pieces fly everywhere. Welcome to my life.

Is it any wonder I struggle with perfectionism as an adult?

I wish I could say my struggle with perfection began with a favorite childhood game. In reality, my perfectionism story probably started in the creation of my DNA. God knew exactly what He was doing when He constructed my detail-oriented, need-for-achievement little brain. He fully intended for me to use that power for good. But the combination of a distinct family structure, combined with a distinct church structure, mixed with various school and work experiences led to a grown woman paralyzed by a mountain of wedding gifts. That was something God had never intended.

A few years ago on my blog, I wrote a series of posts on perfectionism. As a result, I received helpful feedback and comments from readers sharing their own struggles on perfectionism. The process of writing the series and reading the feedback taught me the roots of perfectionism are as unique and personal as each of you.

So, what are the roots? Based on reader comments, my own experience, and a little bit of research, I've come up with the following list.

Temperament:

Certain personality types are more susceptible to perfectionism than others. The temperament of a perfectionist is not erred or flawed. Rather, God gives us our unique temperaments so that we can accomplish our specific purpose on this earth.

Read Romans 12: 3-6 from the Amplified Bible (AMP):

"3 For by the grace (unmerited favor of God) given to me I warn everyone among you not to estimate and think of himself more highly than he ought [not to have an exaggerated opinion of his own importance], but to rate his ability with sober judgment, each according to the degree of faith apportioned by God to him.

4 For as in one physical body we have many parts (organs, members) and all of these parts do not have the same function or use,

5 So we, numerous as we are, are one body in Christ (the Messiah) and individually we are parts one of another [mutually dependent on one another].

6 Having gifts (faculties, talents, qualities) that differ according to the grace given us, let us use them: [He whose gift is] prophecy, [let him prophesy] according to the proportion of his faith..." (emphasis mine)

Our temperament (a combination of our faculties, talents, qualities) is a gift. It's meant to be used for God's glory—to fit within and be mutually dependent upon other members of the Body of Christ. Given a loving and nurturing environment, a detail-oriented, structured, high-achieving personality type will greatly excel in life. (I don't know about you, but some things I really want a detail-oriented, structured, high-achieving person doing for me—performing surgery on my brain, for example.) If you or your child tends toward a perfectionist personality, take heart! It doesn't have to be oppressive.

I have some hard-wiring toward perfectionism, for sure. Two of my children do, as well. To that end, I don't want to try to undo our hard-wiring, but neither do I want us to drag it around through life like a giant bag of trash. I want us to use our God-given temperament for the purpose He intended.

Product of Critical Parent:

According to Clinical Psychologist Dr. Margaret Jordan, *"At the root of perfectionism is usually an early experience in life of not enough reassurance and encouragement, possibly combined with implied or directly stated criticism, blame, or punishment. This kind of start in life, which may even come from well-meaning parents, fosters a feeling of insecurity and the fantasy in the child that if only he or she can do things just right, the parent will be happy, will show love, or will stop the criticism. The child grows up needing evidence from other people of her worth, because she doesn't have an inner sense of being good enough as she is. But no matter how much positive feedback is received, the need is never satisfied, and the insecurity remains."*[12]

Read the following Scriptures concerning fathers speaking harshly to their children, and answer the questions that follow:

Colossians 3:21 (AMP)
21 Fathers, do not provoke or irritate or fret your children [do not be hard on them or harass them], lest they become discouraged and sullen and morose and feel inferior and frustrated. [Do not break their spirit.]

According to this verse, what happens when parents are hard on their kids?

_____

_____
_____

_____

Ephesians 6:4 (AMP)
4 Fathers, do not irritate and provoke your children to anger [do not exasperate them to resentment], but rear them [tenderly] in the training and discipline and the counsel and admonition of the Lord.

Contrast the two parenting styles described in this verse.

_____

_____
_____
_____

_____

Even well-meaning, loving parents can be critical at times and foster perfectionism in children. This was certainly true for me. If this was your experience as a child, keep reading. I offer help to break free and extend forgiveness at the end of this lesson.

Product of a Critical Church Environment:

Similar to a harsh parental environment, a legalistic, rule-based church environment can plant and/or water the seeds of perfectionism.

Read Matthew chapter 23 in your Bible and meet me back here to answer a few questions.

While you were reading, did you notice how Jesus reserved the most severe warnings and harshest language for religious leaders? At the time, these were the teachers of the law and the Pharisees, who placed the heavy burden of rules and regulations onto their followers.

Now, look back at the following verses. Describe the negative impact harsh and legalistic religious leaders can have on those who follow them:

Verse 4:

_____

Verse 13:

_____

Verse 15:

_____

Verse 23:

_____

Legalism is exhausting and toxic. I know, because I was part of a church like this during a significant segment of my life. I was a rule-keeping kind of girl, so I fell easily into the rhythm of a church culture that put a lot of emphasis on keeping rules, both written and implied. I learned early on that people liked me a lot when I dressed a certain way, looked a certain way, and said "yes" to everything that was asked of me. When I had questions—even as an adult—leaders and fellow church members warned me against questioning authority. With my God-given temperament, my home environment, and now my church environment, I was a perfectionism train-wreck waiting to happen.

Fear:

Fear is the root of every Barrier to Balance, as we will see over the coming weeks. At the root of perfectionism is a fear of rejection, a fear of failure, and a fear of punishment. I never considered myself a fearful person, until I began studying this. Perfectionism had such a stronghold on my life. I see now how full of fear I actually was.

In your Bible, read 1 John 4:18. Write out the entire verse here, word-for-word.

_____

_____

_____

Pride:

Pride is also the root of every Barrier to Balance. In fact, I'm going out on a limb here and declaring that, if you are distant from God, fear and/or pride are the culprits. Both are incredibly dangerous to your spiritual health. We must address and expel them at the very first hint of their presence in our hearts.

Regarding perfection, pride whispers the lie that anything other than God can be perfect. Pride also says that we can be what God called us to be through *our* abilities, *our* strengths, *our* efforts, and *our* knowledge.

Read 1 Peter 5:5-6 in your Bible. What does God do to the proud?

_____

_____

What two things does God do to the humble?

But Doesn't God Tell us to be "Perfect?"

This was a question I often wrestled with as a young believer in Christ because of the following verse:

"Be perfect, therefore, as your heavenly Father is perfect." Matthew 5:48

The word translated as "perfect" in this verse is the Greek word *"teleios,"* meaning: *"complete in all its parts, brought to its end, finished, full grown, adult or mature."* It can also be translated *"complete."*

It's the same word translated as "perfect" in 1 John 4:18, the scripture you wrote out on page 95 when you looked at the root of fear.

"There is no fear in love. But perfect love drives out fear, because fear has to do with punishment. The one who fears is not made **perfect** *in love." (emphasis mine.)*

Knowing the full definition of *"teleios,"* now look at Matthew 5:48 in the Amplified Bible:

You, therefore, must be perfect [growing into complete maturity of godliness in mind and character, having reached the proper height of virtue and integrity], as your heavenly Father is perfect.

God is not commanding us to live a life free of mistakes. Neither is He calling us to a life of distress and dysfunction where we strive for an impossible standard. Instead, He calls us to be *complete and mature.*

This maturity is impossible apart from Jesus. It's Christ's perfection working through us that makes this perfection possible. We are complete—made perfect—in Him and through Him.

Look up the following scriptures in your Bible and note the area in which God is calling us to be "perfect":

1 John 4:18: _____

Colossians 3:14 and 1 Corinthians 1:10: _____

2 Corinthians 7:1: _____

Hebrews 12:2: _____ _____

Isaiah 26:3: _____

Perfectionism vs. Excellence

Sometimes the lines of balance become blurred when I confuse the concepts of perfection and excellence. Personally, I experience personal fulfillment from completing tasks well. I have a strong work ethic. I like to do my best. I don't like the thought of people (or God) thinking I've wasted or misused my gifts and talents.

On that glorious day when I finally meet God face-to-face, I don't want Him to look at what I've done with the gifts He has given me and conclude, *"Welp, on a scale of one to ten, you were a solid six. Come now, into the outdated mansion I've prepared for you. It's a fixer-upper, commensurate with your efforts on earth...dark walls, low ceilings, laminate countertops throughout..."*

Wanting to do my best is not a bad thing. Except, as a recovering perfectionist, "my best" sometimes feels like a goal just beyond my reach. No matter what I do, I feel like I could have done better. Often, the only thing that forces Perfectionist Sandy to quit anything is time—simply running out of time.

After nearly every action I perform—a conversation with my husband, a discipline situation with my children, a speaking engagement, a phone call, dinner preparation, bargain hunting, exercise—I walk away and tiny voice inside whispers, *"You could have done better."* This is the typical internal self-talk of a perfectionist.

Look up Colossians 3:23 in you Bible and write it word-for-word here:

_____

_____

_____

As a Christian, I'm called to work at everything with all my heart. I get that. Sometimes, though, I struggle to live this out without striving for perfection.

Can you relate to this? If so, in what ways do you confuse completing tasks with excellence (healthy) versus striving for perfectionism (unhealthy)?

_____

_____

_____

Defining Biblical Excellence

"An excellent wife, who can find? For her worth is far above jewels." Proverbs 31:10 NASB

Ah...the Proverbs 31 woman. Talk about a high standard! Right out of the box, King Lemuel describes her as "excellent."

Awesome, another perfect woman we need to keep up with, right?!

Wrong.

Circle the word "excellent" in Proverbs 31:10 above.

The word translated as "excellent" in this verse is the Hebrew word "*ha-yil.*" It appears 98 times in the Bible, where it is most often used to describe men. Usually, when describing men, the translators chose "*valiant*" or "*able.*" It is sometimes translated as "*riches*" or "*wealth.*" In some places, it's actually translated as "*army*"! (Here is your validation that you are, in fact, doing the work of a hundred people. You're welcome.)

Look at that same verse in a few other translations. Circle the word each translator chose for "ha-yil" instead of "excellent."

AMP: "*An excellent woman [one who is spiritual, capable, intelligent, and virtuous], who is he who can find her? Her value is more precious than jewels and her worth is far above rubies or pearls.*"

KJV: "*Who can find a virtuous woman? for her price is far above rubies.*"

NIV: "*A wife of noble character who can find? She is worth far more than rubies.*"

NLT: "*Who can find a virtuous and capable wife? She is more precious than rubies.*"

YLT: "*A woman of worth who doth find? Yea, far above rubies [is] her price.*"

(I included that last one because I like the word "doth.")

Of the 98 times "ha-yil" appears in the Bible, it is only used two other times to describe women:

Ruth 3:11 (AMP): "a woman of strength—worth, bravery, capability"

Proverbs 12:4 (AMP): "a virtuous and worthy wife—earnest and strong in character."

In every instance, "excellent" describes character and strength—it never describes an outcome. Certainly, God cares about how we do things, whether done well or poorly. He wants us to work with all our hearts for Him, but He's much more concerned with the attitude behind the doing than the actual doing.

Excellence, then is not an endless striving toward "doing my best." Excellence is a pursuit of character qualities and the attributes of God (strength, virtue, love, justice, and mercy), rather than the results of a finished product (a clean house, a well-organized event, the number on the scale).

And—here's the key—acquiring those attributes results not from pursuing the attributes themselves, but from pursuing God. So, by all means, be that woman of excellence God called you to be, by chasing after God's heart.

I have much more to teach you about perfectionism, but this lesson is crazy-long. Let's break here and continue in the next lesson. *Before you go, jot down three things you've learned so far…it doesn't have to be perfect, though.*

1.

2.

3.

Let's pray:

Lord,

I approach Your throne of grace with confidence so that I may receive mercy and find grace to help me in my time of need. Your word says if I hold to Your teaching, I am Your disciple, and that I will know the truth and the truth will set me free. It is for freedom You have set me free. Please set me free from perfectionism.

Help me identify the roots of fear. As I place them under your perfect love, You will cast them out, for Your love casts out all fear. Help me identify the roots of pride, because You resist the proud, but give grace to the humble.

Help me live a life of "perfection" by Your definition: complete and mature in love, in unity, in holiness, in faith, and in peace.

Help me live a life of "excellence" by Your definition: virtuous, capable, and having noble character.

Finally Jesus, whatever I set my hand to do, I will do it with all my might for You and not for any man, past or present.

Thank you for revealing to me everything that hinders me in my quest for balance.

In Jesus' name.

Amen.

LESSON FIVE

Perfectionism, Continued

When Perfectionists Collide

Before I became a Professional Carpool-Driver, Specializing in Efficient Laundry Management, and Healthy Food Preparation for a Family of Five (aka, Mom), I had a job where I got paid real money. In the seven years between college graduation and the birth of my first child, I worked in the claims department for the nation's largest automobile insurance carrier.

If you would have gotten hurt in a car accident that was not your fault, and the at-fault person was insured with our company, I would have been the person ~~you cursed at~~ who handled your claim. (Unless, of course, you believed the commercials that said the insurance company would rip you off. Then I would have been the one who dealt with your attorney—who was more likely to be the one who ripped you off.)

I tell you this because, during my entire seven-year gig, I was at the height of my perfectionism. And for about two of those seven years, I worked for a fellow perfectionist.

A typical work week went like this:

I would receive a new claim and add it to my inventory of hundreds of active claims.

I would work 12-hour days to ensure I did everything I could possibly do to offer the best customer service I knew to offer. I would often leave the office at 7:00 p.m., take files home, and work on the evenings and weekends.

I was never quite satisfied with the quality of my written reports or communication logs, being a perfectionist and all. Since this was my first real job, I set a ridiculously high standard for myself. Anything less than perfect work was completely unacceptable to me. So, I worked longer and harder to make my reports and logs even better.

I would then turn my files in to Perfectionist Boss for weekly review.

He was a nice guy and everything—we actually got along great—but anything less than perfect was unacceptable to him, too. He would meticulously examine each file. Line by line, he would inspect my work. Because he was also a perfectionist, he would find mistakes: bills I should have scrutinized more thoroughly before I paid, liability I assessed before I did a more thorough investigation, vehicle repairs I authorized before I determined they were part of the accident.

I would receive the files back—files I had worked on incessantly and perfectly—and they would be filled with comments, critiques, and instructions to do more. (Cue the pressure in my chest and the pain across my back.)

I would review my files a second time, and set out to do all the things Perfectionist Boss said I needed to do to be perfect. *More* investigation. *More* assessment. *More* documentation.

Then I would resubmit my files, and he would reexamine them. Inevitably, he'd find more mistakes and write more comments, more critiques, and more instructions, causing me more chest pressure and more back pain.

I would review the files, *again*, and set out to do all the things he'd instructed, *again*.

More. More. More.

It never ended. I don't think I ever got a single file back in the two years I worked for him that simply said, "*Well done.*"

One day, while standing at my desk, surrounded by hundreds of files that needed more attention and a stack of un-returned phone messages from attorneys and disgruntled, injured car accident victims, I felt my heart begin to race. A sudden pressure crushed my chest, and I had numbness and tingling down my arms into my hands. I nearly passed out.

I was a healthy, fit, 26-year-old woman, yet the combined pressure of my own impossible standards and the impossible standards of my boss caused my body to rebel. In a stupor, I picked up my purse, walked over to my secretary's desk, and announced I was leaving for the day. Then I drove over to my husband's office and collapsed into his arms, because I did not know if my body could withstand this endless cycle of perfectionism.

I've spent most of this lesson focusing on the pressure we perfectionists put on ourselves, and that is something for which we need to take responsibility. However, it's vital to address the pressure other perfectionists heap on us, as well. For well-functioning, emotionally whole people who do not struggle with perfectionism, pressure from perfectionists is nothing more than a mild irritation. Those people can look a perfectionist in the face and say, "*You're being ridiculous.*" (Well, maybe they don't always say that. Maybe that's just my own little fantasy. That's how I envision the freedom of the non-perfectionist.)

For perfectionists though, that same pressure from a fellow perfectionist becomes more than frustrating. It's frightening. Anxiety is a real problem for perfectionists, and multiplies exponentially when our self-imposed standards collide with the absurd standards of others.

It may not be your boss. Maybe it's a spouse, a parent, a child, or a friend.

Maybe it's a committee leader, a college professor, or a pastor. Perfectionists are everywhere—some of them so entrenched in perfectionism, they need clinical intervention. We're bound to collide with them sooner or later.

So, what's a perfectionist to do when faced with the demands of a fellow perfectionist? Here's what works for me.

1. **Stay filled with God's word.** I can't stress this enough. The Bible not only provides proper perspective, but also the strength we need to endure any trial. (At the end of this lesson, I offer a list of scriptures for meditation and/or memorization and a scripture-based prayer.)

2. **Call it what it is.** If ever the old adage "It takes one to know one" rings true, it's with perfectionists. Because of my own struggles, I can now spot a fellow perfectionist a mile away. I'm learning just how outlandish my own standards are. Now I need to dig deep and find the courage to name it when I see it in others: *This is Perfectionism: an unrealistic, ungodly standard to which I do not need to measure myself, thankyouverymuch.*

3. **Don't argue with the Perfectionist.** Especially if he is your boss. Most perfectionists can't be reasoned out of their dysfunction anyway. This will only lead to more frustration.

4. **Set a healthy boundary.** State your limits clearly and then stick to your guns. *This is what I am able to do.* Period. If the perfectionist does not accept your boundary, distance yourself from the relationship, if you can. (More on all this later in the lesson)

5. **Surround yourself with other people who are not perfectionists.** It is important to interact with emotionally healthy people and glean from their coping strategies. I remember how helpful it was for me to talk to co-workers. Not everyone was working like a dog at my company. It was enlightening to understand how they were able to pull that off. Don't be afraid to ask questions, *"This person expects this of me…is this appropriate in your*

opinion? How would you respond?"

6. **Maintain a variety of healthy interests and relationships**. Spend time away from the criticisms and observations of a fellow perfectionist. Enjoy exercise, hobbies, and recreation. Do things on a regular basis that allow you to get outside of your own head.

7. **Be yourself, no matter how much a perfectionist approves or disapproves of your behavior or performance.** I know this is tough. Especially since people pleasing and perfectionism are so closely related. (I know…can of worms! We will discuss this connection in Lessons Ten and Eleven.)

8. **Seek professional help if you need to**. Talk to someone who understands personality disorders and their detrimental effect on relationships. This is one of the best decisions I've ever made.

After that episode in my office, I sought counsel with my father-in-law, who also happens to be a psychologist. He informed me I had a panic attack due to work stress. (Yes, I needed someone to tell me that! Prior to that, I had never heard of a panic attack.) He offered to write me a prescription and suggested a medical leave of absence from my job. I didn't take him up on his offer, but this was a wake-up call that something was terribly wrong with the relationship dynamic between me and my boss. I had to make a change.

Shortly after the panic attack, Jon and I decided to move from Ohio and relocate to Florida where Jon was taking a new job. We moved to a city where the people moved at a snail's pace compared to my hometown. My company transferred me to an office where my new boss was the polar opposite of Perfectionist Boss. She was a former kindergarten teacher— gentle, nurturing, and easygoing. I never had another work-related panic attack.

I love happy endings, don't you?

As a perfectionist, do you collide with another perfectionist? What is one strategy you can grab from that list and begin implementing immediately to improve your emotional state?

Breaking Through the Barrier of Perfectionism

Do you find your pursuit of balance blocked by the barrier of perfectionism? Let me offer you some hope. A few years ago, I encountered a significant breakthrough in my pursuit of freedom from perfectionism. I had spent months studying perfectionism, writing a blog series about it, and simultaneously putting into practice everything I've written in this lesson. After I was finished, I went to the beach for spring break.

I love the beach. It's my absolute favorite place on Earth. (Disclaimer: I haven't been to a lot of places on Earth, so I reserve the right to change the ranking of the beach should I ever encounter a more favorite place.)

We vacation on the ocean every year. Normally, I spend a lot of time walking the beach, assessing my life. I consider where I am and where I'm going. I examine my heart, my motives, and my actions. I plot out ways to improve myself. I read books in the *Christian-Non-Fiction-Self-Help* genre. I highlight and jot down notes in the sidebar of my self-help books. I pray and journal about all I intend to improve after vacation.

Basically, I strive to be more perfect.

Unplugging my brain—even on the beach—does not come naturally. I fear letting go of my perpetual self-improvement-agenda. I fear not using every opportunity to be the best possible wife, mom, writer, friend, Christian I can be. I fear if I let down my guard—for even just one moment—I will also let down *people*.

You wanna know what I did this particular week—the week after my period of intense work and personal breakthrough?

I unpacked my computer and self-help books, but left them untouched on my side table.

I read two secular books with the spiritual nourishment equivalent of a Twinkie and a packet of Splenda.

I walked on the beach barefoot every morning, not to assess my life, but rather to feel the sand on my feet.

I prayed, but mostly a prayer of gratitude rather than a plea for transformation.

I had dessert and wine with almost every dinner.

I made no self-examinations, no life-altering plans, and no meaningful journal entries.

I did not write.

I did not think.

Well, I did not think beyond, *Hmmmmm... Beach or pool first today?* and *Where are we eating?*

Maybe that describes every vacation for you, but this was the beginning of a major paradigm shift for me. I actually found freedom in setting aside the perpetual self-improvement agenda, embracing my imperfections, and leaning into God's grace.

For the first time in my life, I am completely okay with the fact that I am a flawed human being. I know in the depths of my heart that God actually delights in me—flaws and all. (See Psalm 18:18-20) This process has silenced the voices of my harshest critics—external and internal. I promise, you can also be free from this dysfunctional and debilitating way of thinking.

But how?

Your freedom will require some deep, deliberate, focused work. Here I offer you several strategies I continue to implement to this day. Be patient with yourself as you move through these steps. It may take a while:

1. **Identify the roots of perfectionism**. If you are hard-wired this way, recognize this and embrace it! God wants to use those gifts for His purpose. Beyond that, identify the people, situations, and events that impressed lies on your heart.

Has someone told you, "It's never okay to mess up?" Or "Nothing you do is ever good enough?" Or "If you do all the right things, then you will earn love and acceptance?" If yes, name them.

_____

_____

_____

2. **Forgive the people who you identified**. This is not a one-and-done process. True, lasting forgiveness comes in layers. Forgive what you know to forgive right now, the best you can, but expect that as new situations arise in your life, you will need to forgive again. For example, most of my forgiveness for my parents came after I became a parent myself. It wasn't until I started raising my own children that I realized how my own upbringing had profoundly shaped my perfectionism. As you approach each new situation and discover more roots, forgive again. Be patient with yourself. It's a process.

Forgive the people you named above. Go ahead and grab some tissues. This is hard work. (You're doing a great job, by the way. Keep going.)

3. **Sever or distance yourself from controlling relationships**. If you have people in your life who are critical and/or demanding of you today, you must put good boundaries around yourself. Depending on who the controlling person is, your boundaries will look different. As an adult, boundaries protecting you from a critical parent are going to look different from boundaries protecting you from a critical spouse.

For example, if you still have a relationship with a critical and controlling parent, you may decide you no longer share details about your finances or your marriage, or you may need to stop inviting the parent to your home.

If you are married to a critical spouse, you may need to address specifically what he does to feed your insecurities. You may need to say, *"When you question how much I spend at the grocery store, I feel like I can never get it right. Can we talk about that?"*[14]

Do you need to draw boundaries around any controlling relationships? What will you do this week to begin that process?

_____

_____

_____

_____

_____

4. Establish new habits. Just like an overweight person who begins the journey to health and fitness, she must deal with the root issues. (Why does she have an unhealthy relationship with food? How does she redefine her worth in the light of God's word?) Then she must also break the bad habits that developed as a result of those dysfunctional roots. (She must stop eating junk. She must eat good food in smaller portions. She must exercise, etc.) She has to do both simultaneously, or she will never become healthy and fit—at least not permanently. If she only deals with the roots, but never changes her behavior, she will still be overweight. If she deals with her behavior, but never the root, she risks falling back into old habits.

And so, it is with perfectionists. We must deal with both the roots *and* the behavior to be completely free forever. I, for one, intend to be completely free forever.

Here are some daily habit-changers that work well for me:

- I intentionally silence that inner voice that says, *"You could have done better."* When I hear it, which is still quite often (But less often than I used to hear it), I say in response, *"I did the best I could with what I knew and the time I had."*

- I've learned how a simple timer can be a recovering perfectionist's best friend. I set timers for every task that has the potential to lure me back into perfectionist behavior. (I'm working against a timer now, as I write this lesson!) When the timer goes off, I declare it "good enough."

- For tasks that overwhelm me (Hello, Wedding-Gift-Fiasco!), I practice "Five Minutes or Five Things." This is a technique I read about years ago where I tackle giant projects in very small increments; just five Christmas cards, just five minutes decluttering the closet, etc. Sometimes it's ten minutes or ten things—the number doesn't matter. The idea is that I'm setting mini-goals. I eat away at giant jobs in small portions, a little at a time. I set a timer or a number of things to accomplish and walk away when I've completed that amount. At the risk of sounding over-the-top, this technique is magical. I've discovered I can do *anything* for five or ten minutes. Plus, once I dive in and start eating away at it, the task is never as daunting as I thought it would be. I use this particular technique every single day—it's my favorite perfectionist life hack.

Identify one perfectionist thought pattern or behavior you want to tackle immediately. Name it:

_____

_____

What is one thing you can do beginning today to start forming a new, healthy habit?

_____

_____

5. Replace faulty thought patterns. All barriers begin with a lie—a lie we believe about ourselves, about life, or about God—and all freedom begins with Truth. The only way to truly break through these barriers and be free is to hold each and every lie up to the Truth of God's word. Then, we replace the lie with Truth.

Look up John 8:31-32 in your Bible. Write it here:

_____

_____

_____

_____

So, when you've had lies engraved on your heart (*"It's not okay to mess up." "I am not good enough." "I only matter when I do things well."*), the only thing powerful enough to erase those is the light of God's word.

Invite God's truth into every painful memory—especially the ones from your childhood. Ask God to take the living, active power of His Word and decimate the lies that the Enemy engraved on your tender heart. Ask Him to mend the wounded, confused places that you've carried into adulthood. Ask Him to replace those lies with truth about you, truth about the way the world works, and truth about God.

This can be a very painful process. It involves digging deeply and remembering things you probably don't want to recall. As you do this, you may need to keep moving back through steps 1 and 2 again and again: identifying your roots, remembering early, painful events, forgiving the people who hurt you, and holding it all up to the Light of the Word. All of this should be done in the privacy of your own home or in the hands of a competent Christian counselor.

Don't be discouraged if this takes you a long time. As well-balanced women of God, our goal is growth over time.

If you aren't sure where to start in the scriptures, I've listed some here, along with a Scripture-based prayer. Praying the Word is a powerful tool against the barrier of perfectionism. It will literally change the way you think.

Scriptures for Perfectionists

"See what great love the Father has lavished on us, that we should be called children of God! And that is what we are! The reason the world does not know us is that it did not know him." 1 John 3:1

"Therefore the LORD longs to be gracious to you, And therefore He waits on high to have compassion on you. For the LORD is a God of justice; How blessed are all those who long for Him." Isaiah 30:18

"But where sin increased, grace increased all the more" Romans 5:20

"My grace is sufficient for you, for my power is made perfect in weakness.' Therefore I will boast all the more gladly about my weaknesses, so that Christ's power may rest on me." 2 Corinthians 12:9

"I do not set aside the grace of God, for if righteousness could be gained through the law, Christ died for nothing!" Galatians 2:21

"For it is by grace you have been saved, through faith—and this is not from yourselves, it is the gift of God" Ephesians 2:8

"May our Lord Jesus Christ himself and God our Father, who loved us and by his grace gave us eternal encouragement and good hope," 2 Thessalonians 2:16

"The grace of our Lord was poured out on me abundantly, along with the faith and love that are in Christ Jesus." 1 Timothy 1:14

"He has saved us and called us to a holy life—not because of anything we have done but because of his own purpose and grace. This grace was given us in Christ Jesus before the beginning of time," 2 Timothy 1:9

"Let us then approach God's throne of grace with confidence, so that we may receive mercy and find grace to help us in our time of need." Hebrews 4:16

Before you pray, jot down just three take-aways from this lesson:

1.

2.

3.

Let's pray:

Lord,

I bring before You every painful memory from my past and every person who played a role in those painful memories. For every harsh, hard, or critical word spoken over me, I forgive (name them) today and will continue to forgive as many times as I need to forgive them, until I am free. You have lavished grace on me that I should be called your child. Help me to lavish grace in the same measure on those who hurt me. Where sin increases, let grace increase all the more.

Thank you, Lord that I am fearfully and wonderfully made, having gifts, faculties, talents and qualities that differ from others according to the grace You've given me. Allow me to use those gifts to glorify You and to edify the body of Christ. Thank you for every one of my strengths and weaknesses, for each is divinely placed in me by Your loving hand. Your grace is sufficient for me, for Your power is made perfect in my weakness. Therefore, I will boast all the more gladly about my weaknesses so Your power will rest upon me.

By the power of the name of Jesus and with the authority of Your word, I cancel out every lie I have believed about myself. Let Your truth be the only thing I believe: I am an excellent woman of noble character. I am one who is spiritual, capable, intelligent, and virtuous. I have great worth.

None of this is because of anything I have done, but because of Your own purpose and grace in Christ Jesus. I can cease from striving and enter into Your rest. I do not set aside the grace of God, for if righteousness could be gained through the law, Christ died for nothing. For it is by grace I have been saved, through faith—and this is not from myself, it is the gift of God. The grace of our Lord was poured out on me abundantly, along with the faith and love that are in Christ Jesus.

Help me to set healthy expectations for myself and for others. Help me be gracious to myself when I fail. You long to be gracious to me. You wait on high to be compassionate to me. Help me have the same grace and compassion for myself and for others.

I am free. I walk in freedom and live in freedom. May our Lord Jesus Christ himself and God our Father, who loves us, by his grace give us eternal encouragement and good hope.

In Jesus' name.

Amen.

LESSON SIX

The Comparison Trap

A few years ago, in the dead of a rainy, dreary, cold Kentucky winter, I went searching online for a women's conference to attend. My youngest daughter was still a toddler, which meant most days I was house-bound. My big daily outing was driving my older kids to school. Each day felt like an eternity as winter dragged on. I needed to get out of the house—and not just to the grocery store. I craved a night away in a hotel, in the presence of other (adult) women, minus kids and carpools.

I needed something to nourish and refresh my soul.

So, I clicked around until I found an event that looked like a good fit. It was close enough for me to travel by car, yet far enough that I needed to book a hotel. It was a blogging conference that promised relevant teaching and Christ-centered worship led by women.

It did not involve children.

It did not involve carpools.

It looked perfect.

Then I began reading the speaker bios.

It may have been the cabin fever talking, but every description of the women leading this conference looked like this to me:

Susie Smith is a homeschooling mother of six. She and her husband live on a farm, where she creates nightly meals from scratch with the organic vegetables she has grown and harvested with her bare hands. Her passions include, home interior design, green living, frugal living, women's ministry, and nurturing sick and orphaned animals back to health. She is the author of seven books and the wildly popular blog, I Have It All Together, Why Don't You?

(Insert professional headshot of beautiful, flawless woman, on a farm)

Jenny Jones has lived in seven countries and dreams of living in five more. She is a homeschooling mother of four; ages nine, eight, seven, and six. She and her husband are expecting quadruplets in the fall. She is a marathon runner and plans to complete her 5th marathon just before delivering the quads. She has led over 50,000 people to Christ, through her personal discipleship and mentoring program. In her spare time, she enjoys creating gourmet recipes for her best-selling cookbooks and has appeared on The Food Network, The Today Show, Oprah, *and* Ellen.

(Insert professional headshot of beautiful, flawless, buff woman—who looks neither pregnant nor tired.)

Ugh.

I'm exaggerating about the content of the bios, but not about the inadequacy I felt as I read them. It appeared that each woman speaking at this conference was simply unbelievable. I wish I could say I acted like a grown-up and celebrated each woman's accomplishments as I considered how I might glean something of worth from her, but that would be a lie. Instead, I was jealous. With every bio, I compared that woman's accomplishments to my own and mine fell painfully short:

Sandy Cooper is a stressed-out mom of three. She knows she could never home school because she can barely handle the stress of doing math homework with her 4ᵗʰ grader, during which she enjoys sampling "calming teas." In her spare time, she folds laundry. Every morning, she wakes up wondering how she's going to get it all done, and most days, she doesn't. She loves to write, but mostly uses her gift to craft daily to-do lists. She's not sure if her kids actually brush their teeth, and last week, she packed a sandwich in her daughter's lunch with the wrapper still on the cheese. Her roots are growing in. She dreams of changing the world, but neglects changing dead light bulbs, dirty bed sheets, and the kitty litter.

(Insert un-touched photo of me in yoga pants, ponytail, and no make-up)

After my brutal exercise in self-deprecation, I simply didn't measure up. The more I read and compared, the more defeated and deflated I became. Eventually, I clicked off the website, turned off my computer, and shuffled my pathetic, underachieving-self into bed. I never booked the conference. So much for "nourish and refresh my soul."

If one thing universally messes with our balance as women, it's comparison to other women. The older I get, and the more other women my age accomplish in life, the more brutal the comparison trap becomes for me. Sometimes I feel like everyone is dashing past me, doing all the things I envision for myself—things I thought I would have already accomplished by now. Yet, here I am, limping breathlessly behind, buried under a pile of laundry or stuck in a carpool line.

Maybe you aren't comparing yourself to writer/speaker/moms, like I am, but you are comparing yourself to...

The neighbor with the beautifully decorated, always immaculate home.

The couple in your church with the thriving, healthy marriage.

That family on your Facebook feed with the polite, intelligent, and spiritually mature children.

The entrepreneur generating a 6-figure income in her jammies.

The retired woman in your book club who is traveling through Europe.

To us, they appear perfect, or near-perfect. We see them. We envy them. We wonder what we are doing wrong. And then, we erect a ridiculously high standard with which we feel compelled to judge ourselves.

Ladies, this is a terribly dangerous place to linger.

I have never met a woman who does not struggle with comparison on some level. What about you? Does this barrier pose a problem for you and your balance? *Rate yourself on a scale of 1 to 10.*

Comparison is not a problem for me ------------------------*Comparison paralyzes me*

| 1 | 2 | 3 | 4 | 5 | 6 | 7 | 8 | 9 | 10 |

Who are the people you compare yourself to most often? Name them here. We will refer to these names later. (You can use code words if you think someone may see this—that's what I do):

_____

_____
_____

_____

The History of The Comparison Trap

The Comparison Trap has been around since the beginning of time, literally. *Read the Bible passages referenced below and answer the questions that follow.*

1. Cain and Abel *Genesis 4:1-8*

Why was Cain jealous of Abel (vv. 3-5)?

_____

Write verse 7 word-for-word.

_____

_____

According to verse 7, how did God give Cain a chance to make it right?

_____

_____

What did Cain do instead? (vs. 8)

_____

_____

Notice that Cain was jealous of Abel because Abel chose to obey God and God granted Abel with favor. Do you ever feel jealous of other women because they are doing the God-honoring thing, and you are not?

_____

_____

_____

_____

Comparison leads to jealousy and jealousy is sin. I love the way God refuses to dance around this issue with Cain. He basically says, *"What is your problem, Cain? Why are you so angry with your brother? If you do what I ask you to do, I will accept your sacrifice, too!"* Then, God directly warns, *"But if you do not do what is right, sin is crouching at your door; it desires to have you,* **but you must rule over it."**

Comparison is a slippery slope. For Cain, what started as feelings of anger and sadness (vs. 6) quickly escalated to murder! This is why we must gain control over it at the very first hint.

Okay, so my jealousy has never resulted in murder—I'm hoping yours has not either. Still, it's alarming how closely the two are related in this example. *How else might you harm someone when you become jealous of them?*

_____

_____

What are some practical ways you can "rule over" or control the temptation to compare yourself to other women before you harm them?

_____

_____

_____

_____

2. Saul and David *1 Samuel 16:14-23, 1 Samuel 18:5-12*

How is David described at the time he met Saul? What kind of young man was he? (1 Sam 16:18)

_____

_____

How did Saul feel about David when he first met him? (1 Sam 16:21-22)

_____

_____

When and why did Saul begin to feel jealous of David? (1 Sam 18:6-8)

_____

_____

How did Saul's jealously quickly spiral out of control? (1 Sam 18:10-11)

_____

_____

How long did it take between the time Saul became jealous and the time he tried to kill David? (Again, with the murder!) (1 Sam 18:10)

_____

_____

Write 1 Samuel 18:12 word-for-word.

_____

_____

_____

_____

Name the two emotional ways Saul's jealously manifested. (1 Sam 18:8 and 1 Sam 18:12)

_____

_____

When David first came under service to Saul, he met Saul's need. This greatly pleased Saul. David was loyal to his post and loyal to the Lord. His dedication and success opened the doors to more opportunities. Everyone loved David. Every place David served, he excelled, and the people noticed. This is precisely where things took a wrong turn in Saul's attitude.

Do you know a person (maybe a co-worker or family member) who is loyal, dedicated, and well-liked by others? How do you feel about this person when others sing her praises in front of you—or to you?

_____

_____

_____

_____

What about people who seem to do the wrong things (maybe they are dishonest or lack integrity), yet they appear to be winning at life? How do you feel when these people excel past you?

_____

_____

_____

_____

Negative feelings indicate a deeper heart issue. Take a moment to examine your heart. If you feel anger or sadness when others are spoken well of, what could be the deeper issue? (There is no wrong answer here.)

_____

_____

_____

_____

Jews and Paul and Barnabas *Acts 13:42-45*

What were Paul and Barnabas doing at the synagogue? (vv. 42-44)

_____

_____

Why did the Jews become jealous? (vv. 44-45)

_____

_____

What did the Jews do as a result of their jealousy? (vs. 45)

_____

_____

Notice the pattern in these Biblical examples:

Person A obeys God.
Person B disobeys God.
Person A wins the favor of God and/or men because of his obedience.
Person B becomes jealous of Person A.
Person B attempts to harm Person A.

Look back at the names (or code names) of the people you mostly compare yourself with. Do any of them fit the profile of Person A—the one who obeys God?

_____

_____

Do you fit the profile of Person B—the one who is jealous of Person A?

_____

_____

The Comparison Trap Today

Even as recently as 150 years ago, our knowledge of others existed because of our day-to-day interactions with them. We farmed together, shopped together, and raised our kids together in community. (And by "we," I mean "other people." I was not alive when "we" were farming together.) Without cars, airplanes, television, or computers, we had almost no knowledge of those outside our immediate social circle. Because the communities were small, our neighbors were also our kids' classmates, our church family, and our extended family. We saw everything about everyone, good and bad.

I imagine life was a bit more authentic than it is today. After all, how can you possibly hide behind a façade when the same people surround you day-in-and-day-out? Your dirty laundry hangs out for all to see—*literally*.

Today, our knowledge of others is quite the opposite. **Instead of knowing a few people intimately, we "know" thousands of people superficially**. Oddly, we know as much about Beyoncé as we do about that mom at our kids' school (who could, quite possibly, be Beyoncé, depending on where your kid goes to school). Our knowledge of everyone comes through a series of virtual snapshots—hundreds and hundreds by the minute: a news quip on our homepage, a Facebook status, a Tweet, an Instagram photo, a Snapchat. How close to reality can this possibly be?

The answer: *not very*.

Today we feed ourselves a steady diet of trivial information on other people, yet lack depth with most of them. Never in the history of humans is it easier for us to see what everyone else is up to (or what they appear to be up to), and then to compare ourselves to it.

As if that isn't bad enough, our minds play a trick on us. We see one woman doing crafts with her toddler, another on a ski vacation with her husband, another selling skin care products on her side hustle, and another doing yoga while diffusing essential oils. We take all the separate images of individual women, and we merge them into one perfect woman. We believe everyone else is doing All The Things, and we judge ourselves against this imaginary standard.

Our hyper-connected society sets us up to crash into this barrier all day, every day.

Less Than

In the first century, the Apostle Paul travelled extensively, spreading the Gospel. While many followed and loved Paul, others strongly opposed him. The false teachers of his day tried to discredit him by questioning his message, his tactics, and his apostolic authority. Paul, speaking under divine inspiration (and with a hint of sarcasm), says of them,

"Oh, don't worry; we wouldn't dare say that we are as wonderful as these other men who tell you how important they are! **But they are only comparing themselves with each other, using themselves as the standard of measurement. How ignorant!"** *2 Corinthians 10:12 (NLT).* (emphasis mine)

These false teachers acted as though the highest standard of behavior was themselves, and then they compared everyone, including Paul, to that standard. Paul called that comparison "ignorant."

The NRSV says, *"they do not show good sense."*

The NIV says, *"they are unwise."*

The Message says, *"they quite miss the point."*

Yes, comparing ourselves to each other is all those things: ignorant, unwise, and quite missing the point. Comparing ourselves to each other is like aiming at a moving target—unsteady and ever-changing. No matter how good we get at something, we can always find someone else who does it better, leaving us feeling perpetually inadequate.

This is not only unhealthy, but also sinful. When God warned against the sin of idol worship (Exodus 20), He wasn't only referring to images carved from gold or wood. **He was referring to looking to** *anyone or anything other than God* **as a standard of measurement.**

Who or what is your standard of measurement? In other words, when you consider

"success" in an area of your life (maybe parenting, marriage, ministry, or fitness) who or what do you envision? If it's a person, name the person. If it's a combination of images, describe the images:

_____

_____

_____

_____

Greater Than

Not all comparison leaves us feeling inadequate, though. Sometimes, we look around and get an inflated opinion of ourselves. We think, *"at least my kids don't do THAT!"* or *"My house isn't as gross as HERS!"* We compare ourselves to others in order to feel better about ourselves. Even that is sin.

In your Bible, read Luke 18:9-14 and answer the following questions.
Describe the people Jesus was talking to in this passage (vs. 9)

_____

_____

Write verse 14 word-for-word.

_____

_____

_____

_____

We can technically do all the "right things," but **as soon as we use *ourselves* as a standard of measurement for righteousness, it becomes pride.**

In your Bible read Jeremiah 9:24 and 1 Corinthians 1:31. According to these verses, what is the only type of "boasting" God allows?

_____

_____

So, either way, whether judging ourselves inadequate or superior, less than or greater than, whenever we compare ourselves to others, it is sin. The comparison trap is like a mirage: it keeps us moving toward something that appears alluring but actually lacks all substance. It's impossible to pursue an ungodly, ever-changing standard and also maintain peace, freedom, or balance.

Thank God, we have the tools to break down this barrier. In the next lesson, we will examine these tools, one-by-one, and learn how to use them.

As always, before you move on, write down three things you want to remember from this lesson:

1. _____

2. _____

3. _____

Let's pray:

Dear Jesus,

Comparing myself with others and using anything but You as a standard of measurement is foolish and prideful. Sin desires to have me, but I must rule over it. You are the God of peace, and You have equipped me with everything good for doing Your will. You are working in me what is pleasing to You. If I boast, I will only boast about this: That I have the understanding to know You, the Lord, Who exercises kindness, justice and righteousness on earth.

Thank you for teaching me how to be completely free from everything that hinders me, even the Comparison Trap.

In Jesus' name,

Amen.

LESSON SEVEN

The Comparison Trap, Continued

My 10-year-old daughter, Elliana, loves to sing, and she's quite good at it. She has perfect pitch and can recall song lyrics like nobody's business. I'm not exaggerating. She can hear a song once and sing it from memory. Her talent is impressive, and she knows it. (This may or may not have something to do with the fact that I tell her she's a good singer approximately 800 times a day.) She's always been comfortable in her skin, but not in an arrogant way. She's simply a carefree kid with a healthy dose of self-confidence, not yet jaded by how her gifts and talents may compare to the gifts and talents of her peers.

That is, until I showed her a viral video on the Internet.

It was two-minute compilation of a little girl saying and doing hilarious things, one of which was singing a short, five-second song. As I was laughing hysterically at the precocious little girl (who also had obvious vocal talent), I looked over at Elliana, and she was frowning. I paused the video and said, *"What's up?"*

She said, *"This video makes me feel bad about myself."*

What? No! Why?

(This is reminiscent of her mother after reading conference speaker bios.)

I looked her in the eye and said, *"Hey, just because this little girl has talent, it doesn't mean you don't."* Then I put my arm around her, winked and said, *"In fact, with 7 billion people in the world, it's very possible more than one of you can sing."*

She nodded, measuring carefully what I said against her visceral response.

You guys, what in the holy heck was that? Are we now starting this crazy comparison game at age 10? I thought I had until middle school (at least) before we would begin trudging through this garbage. This incident made me more determined than ever to bust this barrier before it grows any bigger in her heart.

Breaking Down the Barrier of Comparison

Clearly, comparison at any age and in any form is toxic. Everything from the roots from which it sprouts to the fruit it produces is contrary to God and His purpose. But here is good news: God has given us the tools to break down this barrier so we can live well-balanced lives, free from comparison.

"We use our powerful God-tools for smashing warped philosophies, tearing down barriers erected against the truth of God, fitting every loose thought and emotion and impulse into the structure of life shaped by Christ. Our tools are ready at hand for clearing the ground of every obstruction and building lives of obedience into maturity." 2 Corinthians 10:5 (MSG)

As a woman, I'm regularly running into this barrier right along with you (and my 10-year-old, apparently). I need to confront it daily and deliberately. Let's examine several strategies you can use to walk in freedom.

1. Realize it's not about them; it's about me.

The first step in destroying this barrier is to stop playing the blame game. It's tempting to look around and blame someone else (*She flaunts her perfection in my face*) or blame circumstances (*Nothing good happens for me like it does for her*). However, the responsibility for slipping into comparison rests squarely on our shoulders.

Look back at the Biblical examples we read in Lesson Six (Cain, Saul, the abusive Jews, the men in Corinth opposing Paul, the Pharisee in the midst of his "prayer.") Are there any situations where God sympathized with the person comparing himself to others?

2. Consider the Roots of Comparison.

Sometimes comparison is plain old jealousy: We want what someone else has. This is what happened when Saul heard the women chanting, "*Saul has slain his thousands and David his ten of thousands.*" Even though Saul achieved his own level of success, he wanted the accolades attributed to David.

Sometimes comparison is misplaced guilt: God has instructed us to do something, but we have not done it. Then when we see others doing the very thing we are neglecting to do, it triggers our conscience. Instead of recognizing the warning sign and obeying God, we feel anger toward the other person. This is what happened with Cain and Abel.

Sometimes comparison is misplaced focus: We've forgotten what God has told us to do. This is what happened to me when I read all the stellar bios for the women's conference speakers. At the time, I had three young children at home. God was not telling me to homeschool, travel, speak, write books, or even grow my own vegetables—not during that season. God had clearly called me to transition my newly adopted toddler into our family. He had called me to set aside my writing goals in order to take care of my young children. He called me to be present at home while my husband worked to provide financially for us. All of this meant being mostly house-bound, doing lots of laundry, and running daily carpool. I was squarely in the center of God's will for my life. Had I remembered that, I could have read the women's bios, felt secure in my season, and booked my hotel.

Think about the person or standard to which you most often compare yourself. What is/are the root(s) of that comparison? (Circle all that apply and then explain)

Jealousy   *Misplaced Guilt*   *Misplaced Focus*

_____

_____

_____

3. Keep Your Focus.

My teenaged son is obsessed with cars. Every time we drive together he's constantly pointing and saying, *"Mom! Look at the Corvette! Mom! There's a vintage Cadillac! Mom! There's the Camaro I want!"*

No matter how stellar my driving skills, if I were to take my eyes off the road every time he said, *"Mom, LOOK,"* I'd be swerving everywhere. I'm constantly reminding my son, *"I'm sure that's a cool car, but I'm driving. I need to keep my eyes on the road."*

Whether intentional or not, I drift in the direction I am looking.

This is precisely what happens when we start looking around at other women. If we look away from our goals and our course and instead look at *their* goals and *their* course, we unintentionally start drifting toward it.

I've done it time and time again, especially while scrolling through social media. Just this morning before sitting down to write this lesson, I looked briefly at Instagram. I saw one woman who is currently traveling the world with her husband and children. (She's in Hawaii right now, and her kids are attending virtual school.) Another one moved to South Florida a few years ago and recorded her children frolicking in the waves. Another hosts a popular podcast. Another curled her daughter's hair and took pictures of it. And still another opened her own local boutique last year and just received in stock new must-have jeans.

That was literally what came across my Instagram feed in the last 30 seconds.

If I'm not vigilant about keeping my eyes on my own lane, I will start veering toward those things—at least in my mind. (*We need to travel the world; we need to move back to Florida; I need to start a podcast; I should curl Elliana's hair tonight; I should start my own business; I need new jeans...*) Then, when I turn off my phone and sit down to do *the actual thing God has called me to do* (namely, write this Bible Study!), I feel discontent, sad, and confused. (Ask me how I know this.)

No wonder excessively viewing social media produces so much anxiety in us!

Read Proverbs 4:25-27 in your Bible. According to this passage, where should we be looking? In what direction should we be moving?

_____

_____

_____

As much as I may admire your exceptional running skills, it's not my job to run your race. Neither is it your job to run mine. As soon as we start looking around at what everyone else is doing, we risk getting tangled up in the distraction and falling flat on our faces.

"Therefore then, since we are surrounded by so great a cloud of witnesses [who have borne testimony to the Truth], let us **strip off and throw aside every encumbrance (unnecessary weight) and that sin which so readily (deftly and cleverly) clings to and entangles us, and let us run with**

patient endurance and steady and active persistence the appointed course of the race that is set before us. Looking away [from all that will distract] to Jesus, Who is the Leader and the Source of our faith [giving the first incentive for our belief] and is also its Finisher [bringing it to maturity and perfection]. He, for the joy [of obtaining the prize] that was set before Him, endured the cross, despising and ignoring the shame, and is now seated at the right hand of the throne of God. Hebrews 12:1-2 (AMP) (emphasis mine)

According to Hebrews 12:1-2, what do unnecessary weights and sin do to us when we run?

Imagine that you are a marathon runner. What would happen if something clung to your legs and entangled you while you were racing?

According to this passage, how are we to run our appointed course?

Complete this sentence: "Looking away [from all that will distract] ____ _____, Who is the Leader and the Source of our faith"

If all my friends are looking to Jesus, and I am looking to Jesus, it doesn't matter if we are doing different things. In fact, we absolutely *should be* doing different things—this is how the Church works best. We should all be in our own lanes, running our own race, using our own unique talents—looking to Jesus.

In your Bible, read Ephesians 4:14-17.

What are some of the benefits of each part of the body doing its work?

---

4. Realize You Are Not Supposed to Be Her.

I have a friend who has a beautifully decorated and immaculate home. Seriously, I'm not exaggerating. It's always spotless. Even she admits this. She's not like a crazy person either—she's very relaxed about it all. She has three kids, just like I do. In fact, her kids are much younger than mine. (Usually, younger kids = messier house. Nope. Not with this friend.) And—get this—our houses are not only the same size, but they are the *exact same floor plan*.

I used to wonder what was wrong with me—why I couldn't keep my home as clean as she kept hers. Once, I even called her to ask her about her exact cleaning schedule. I wrote it all down, and then tried to implement it into my week. No lie, I felt like I was killing myself all day to get to a place that seemed to come so effortlessly to her. Even after that, my house still never looked as good as hers.

Then, one day in passing conversation, she described her husband as a "neat freak." As in, he cleans stuff without being asked. Having a spotless home is a high priority for *both of them*, and they *both clean* and work to improve the appearance of their home *on a daily basis*.

Hello.

See, my husband is many things—wise, athletic, hard-working, loyal, handsome, strong, gentle—but "neat-freak," ain't one of them. Sure, given the choice between clean and dirty, he'd mostly choose clean. Sure, he will gladly help me clean something if I ask him, but most of the time, he doesn't even see the dirt or clutter.

That was the day I stopped comparing myself to my friend. That was the day I stopped comparing my house to hers. That was the day I stopped asking myself what I was doing "wrong" because the one and only time my house has ever looked like hers was when we were showing it to prospective buyers to sell it.

As it turns out, I'm not doing anything wrong. She has a different husband than I have, and that *one thing* is the difference between her clean house and my not-so-clean house.

I have another friend. She loves to live a fast-paced life, scheduled down to the minute. When I think of high-output people, I think of this friend. She accomplishes all things at warp speed. She cleans fast. She cooks fast. She drives fast. She walks fast. I've spent a lot of time with her, and I literally run to keep up with her.

I used to beat myself up because I wasn't more like her. When we'd chat about our day and what we accomplished, my list was always smaller, even on my best days.

My "ah-ha" moment came when I realized that I'm at my worst when I feel hurried and rushed. The times when I've chased my friend around, she leaves energized while I leave exhausted. I am not a high-output person. Sure, I love productive days. It's fun to scratch a bunch of things off the list. My most balanced days, though, are those with wide margins built in. I like structure, but I hate scheduling anything down to the minute. I prefer to be very flexible, so I can linger over a task, or over a conversation, or over my cup of coffee. I will never accomplish what she accomplishes in a day because God didn't make me that way. That pace is extremely uncomfortable for me.

God equipped my friend to do the work He has called her to do—she has multiple balls in the air, and she loves it that way. When she's busy, she's in her wheelhouse. In the same way, God has equipped me to do the work He has called me to do. When I'm busy, I'm in the crazy house. Just as I could not sustain her fast pace, she could not sustain my slower one. We are not wired the same way *on purpose.*

Breaking through the barrier of comparison sometimes means I have to remember the "perfect person" to which I'm comparing (and falling short) is simply *not me.* She doesn't have my husband, my temperament, my kids, my home, my gifts, my talents, my weaknesses, or my God-given calling.

In your Bible read Hebrews 13:20-21, and write it here word-for-word:

_____

_____

_____

_____

God has equipped you to live *your life*, not the life of your friend, your sister, or your mother. The same is true for her: God equipped your friend, your sister, and your mom to live *their lives*, not yours. Yet for each of you, God has given exactly what you need—everything good— for doing His will.

"Since this is the kind of life we have chosen, the life of the Spirit, let us make sure that we do not just hold it as an idea in our heads or a sentiment in our hearts, but work out its implications in every detail of our lives. That means we will not compare ourselves with each other as if one of us were better and another worse. We have far more interesting things to do with our lives. Each of us is an original. Galatians 5:25-26 (MSG)

List your best qualities here—the things that make you "an original":

_____

_____

_____

_____

Choose a person you love and also encounter often (your spouse, best friend, sister, etc.). How are you different from him or her? How can you celebrate those differences instead of judging yourself inadequate against him or her?

_____

_____

_____

_____

5. Realize She Isn't Actually Perfect.

Have you ever watched a teenage girl prepare to post a picture on

Instagram? My daughter and her friends will sometimes take 50 pictures of the exact same thing before they select one worthy of posting.

Then they use multiple picture-editing apps to alter the selected image. I've watched my daughter whiten her teeth, darken her hair, and blur the background of photos.

Often before deciding on a caption for the edited photo, she will survey her friends via text to get the wording just right. (Her captions are usually hilarious) Then, and only then, will she post the final product.

It doesn't end there, however. After all that effort, if the picture does not get enough likes in enough time (I'm not sure the proper criteria for determining "enough"), she will delete it.

I am not criticizing my daughter for doing this. I am guilty of similar behavior. While I may not whiten my teeth, I do blur out moles and wrinkles on my face (#oldpeopleproblems). I only post pictures of myself wearing make-up and looking relatively attractive. I may post a family "update," but I assure you, it's never concerning the giant fight I'm having with my husband or the messy details of parenting my teens.

I suppose, for those who follow me on social media, it would be tempting to conclude I always wear make-up, don't have a mole above my left eye, always look cute, and never have fights with my husband.

None of this is remotely true.

Yet, in an effort to protect my family's privacy and filter out ugly pictures, I have unintentionally curated a public image of perfection.

If this is true for me, it's probably true for others. I need to remind myself, over and over, what I see projected in my brief and limited encounters with individuals is not the fullness of reality for them and therefore, is not something to which I need to compare or judge the fullness of my reality.

Lysa Terkeurst says,

"We like to identify our shortcomings, form them into a club, and mentally beat the tar out of ourselves. Over and over and over again. We label ourselves and soon lose our real identity to the beaten and bruised fragility we call 'me.' We compare, we assume, we assess, we measure, and most times walk away shaking our head at how woefully short our "me" falls when compared to everyone else. How dangerous it is to hold up the intimate knowledge of our imperfections against the outside packaging of others."17

It's not only social media. Even our face-to-face interactions are brief and surface-level, mostly. We're too busy, too isolated. When people ask, *"How are you?"* our response is, *"Fine"* whether we're fine or not. It's easy to project a flawless image in the pew of a two-hour church service, or the bleachers of a one-hour soccer game, or the table of a 45-minute business luncheon.

If we appear perfect to others (when we're not), it's fair to assume the perfection we see in others is also not real.

Sometimes, when I'm groveling in comparison, I not only believe other women (moms in particular) are perfect, but I actually convince myself I'm the only mom in the world who is picking smelly socks up off the floor, cooking (again!), or wiping urine off a toilet seat. This is crazy town!

Unless she's paying someone else to do it, every woman is doing laundry, preparing meals, and wiping messes—especially moms. All other people—even the ones to whom I have unfairly compared myself—have flaws and weaknesses, whether I see them or not. Sure, some are better at hiding them than others, but all of them struggle in some area of life. Every woman has insecurities and fears. In fact, some of the "flawless" women in my life probably flounder in areas where I excel.

Consider your interactions with the following people in your life. How might you be projecting an altered or flawless image to these people?

A. Your "friends" and "followers" on social media:

_____

_____

B. Your neighbors:

_____

_____

C. Your co-workers:

_____

_____

D. Your church family:

_____

_____

E. Your extended family:

_____

_____

F. Parents of your children's friends:

_____

_____

What are some ways you can begin showing a more authentic version of yourself to others while still remaining tactful and honoring your family and their privacy?

_____

_____

_____

_____

Do you project an image of perfection onto others? In other words, do you sometimes believe that people in your life are "perfect" or "flawless" or "don't have any problems"? How has the insight gained from this lesson changed your perspective about other people?

_____

_____

_____

_____

6. Be Careful What You Put Before Your Eyes.

About a year ago, I cancelled my subscription to my favorite fitness magazine.

I love reading fitness magazines. I enjoy keeping up on the latest health trends, and I'm a big fan of transformation stories. But after paging through the flawless photos in these magazines, I'd often feel fat and ugly.

It's silly, really. First, because I know I'm not fat or ugly. Second, because I know how fake those pictures are. I've heard numerous fitness celebrities discuss the grueling process of "dieting down" before a photo shoot—some of them even refuse to drink water for an entire day in order to better accentuate muscle tone. I realize models and celebrities spend hours in "hair and make-up" before a photo is taken. I also know that, after all that, photos are digitally manipulated to remove every blemish, wrinkle, and stray hair, and to make skinny girls look even skinnier. By the time I see that picture of those chiseled abs, it amounts to little more than a cartoon.

I know all of this with my logical mind.

Yet when I look at pictures in fitness magazines, I immediately begin comparing my body to the bodies in the pictures—the cartoonish, dehydrated, starved bodies—and, I look very imperfect by comparison.

Read Matthew 6:22-23 and write it here word-for-word.

What you allow in through your eyes eventually takes up residence in your heart. What lives in your heart eventually affects everything.

What most captures your attention when you have free time? What do you watch on TV? What books do you read? What are you viewing on the Internet? When you pick up your phone, what app do you usually open first?

In your Bible, read Proverbs 4:23 and write it here in your own words:

Have you ever felt chronic low-level anxiety? The kind that flies just below your radar all the time? You know it's there, but you aren't quite sure the cause. Perhaps this angst is a result of what you allow into your heart through your eyes.

Maybe for you it isn't the fitness models, but it's the decorating magazines or the cooking websites. I know many women who can't spend time on Pinterest because they feel like they can't keep up with the perfection. Several of my friends have deleted their Facebook accounts because the incessant scrolling through other people's lives makes them feel "yuck" inside. A few years ago, I stopped looking at catalogues altogether. When my husband asked me why they went straight from the mailbox into the recycle bin, I said, "They make me discontent with what I have." I compare my stuff to the stuff in the catalogues and it doesn't measure up—*I don't measure up.*

When anything starts producing unnecessary guilt inside me for failing to keep up, I've discovered it's best to look the other way rather than allow it to suck the life out of me.

"I will set no worthless or wicked thing before my eyes.
I hate the practice of those who fall away [from the right path];
It will not grasp hold of me." Psalm 101:3 (AMP)

In that verse, circle the word "worthless."

Now, underline the last sentence.

What worthless thing can you eliminate from your viewing before it grasps hold of you?

_____

_____

7. Be a Life-Giver, Not a Life-Sucker.

Just as we want to eliminate the things that suck the life from us, we also want to stop being the one who sucks the life out of others.

Remember when we looked at Isaiah 58 in Lesson Two? We're revisiting that chapter, except this time, we're focusing on the portion that deals with comparison.

In your Bible, read Isaiah 58: 9-12

Write out verse 9 word for word:

_____

_____

_____

_____

_____

Comparison is like a yoke of oppression. Holding others to a standard and judging ourselves against it (either greater than or lesser than) is bondage. We can't be truly free while we are dragging around this heavy burden. We invite others into our bondage—placing our yoke directly upon them—when we speak maliciously about those to whom we compare.

This passage says we can choose a different way. We can speak life instead of death. **When we choose to stop participating in negative conversations, and instead, shift our focus to serving others and building each other up, we become life-givers.**

What if, when we see an amazing woman, running her race well, instead of saying, "*I stink*" or "*She stinks!*" we say, "*Good for her!*" What if we cheer her on?

What if, when we see the mom with the great kids, instead of resenting her or avoiding her or secretly hoping you find out her perfect kids do drugs, we say, "*Wow, you must be doing a great job. I could learn so much from you.*"

What if, when we see the friend with the great marriage, instead of trashing her behind her back or wishing we had her perfect husband, we say, "*Your relationship is such an inspiration. Thank you for the great example. Will you pray for my marriage?*"

What if, when we walk into our neighbor's beautifully decorated home, instead of gossiping about how she has too much time on her hands and money to burn, we say to her, "*What a warm, welcoming place you are creating here. It's lovely.*"

What if we decide we are only going to say those things and *think those things* that show love and bring hope, comfort, and healing?

With every interaction, what if we disciplined ourselves to speak life into the situation? Do you see how this would change everything?

Look at verses 10-12. List all the benefits of changing the way we speak and focusing instead on serving others:

_____

_____

_____

_____

_____

8. Ask a Better Question in Your Gratitude Journal.

The foundation of a peaceful, well-balanced mind is the discipline of gratitude. **It's hard to be grateful for what you have and be focused on what you don't have at the same time.**

In your Bible, look up Philippians 4:6-7 and summarize it here:

_____

_____

_____

_____

_____

Everyone from the Apostle Paul to Oprah Winfrey admonishes us to be thankful. If you do an Internet search with the words "gratitude journal" you will find over 6,000,000 results, ranging from actual journals that say "Gratitude" on the cover, to gratitude apps for your smart phone, to psychological studies linking gratitude journals to happiness.

Gratitude journals are insanely popular because they are an effective way to practice the discipline of thankfulness. That is why it frustrates me to no end that I stink at keeping a gratitude journal. Oh, I journal daily, mind you. I write about my day, my goals, my prayers, my struggles. The literal Gratitude Journal, though—this I can't keep. I've given it a good effort. I've tried keeping one special journal that's solely devoted to gratitude. I've tried writing three things a day at the beginning of my journal-journal. I've tried keeping my journal-journal open and on the counter, so I can write things every time I walk by. Nothing sticks.

I've tried buying a Gratitude Journal for our entire family, which sat in the center of our table with a pen attached for a whole year. One year, I tried keeping a "Gratitude Jar" where I asked my family to jot down what they were thankful for on little slips of paper, with the intention of reading them on Thanksgiving.

While amusing, neither captured the sentiment I was going for. My kids wrote things like, *"I'm thankful for swag"* and *"I'm thankful for the coming day when school will become illegal in all states and wiped from existence"*.[18]

Even in my own journal, I couldn't quite figure it out. Like most people, I'd ask myself, *"What am I thankful for?"* And then I'd make a list: *Jesus, Jon, the kids, my home, coffee.*

And the next day: *Jon, kids, coffee, Jesus, my home.*

And the next: *Coffee, Jesus, coffee*

Then I thought it would be better if I went into more detail: *Jesus saving me and giving me peace; a faithful, loving husband who provides for our family; Rebekah's wit; Elijah's enthusiasm; Elliana's joy; my beautiful, comfortable, warm house; morning coffee; afternoon coffee; coffee with cream.*

That is okay, I guess, but seriously, how many times can I write the exact same things? And why does "coffee" appear in my gratitude journal more than people? I am beyond thankful for so many things. I enjoy writing, and I love words. So, why can't I consistently capture in words the things for which I am thankful in a way that accurately reflects my heart?

After much analysis, as to why Operation Gratitude Journal has failed to stay afloat, I've concluded that I have been asking the wrong question.

Instead of "What am I thankful for?" I decided to start asking, "What do I want to remember, forever and ever, about yesterday?"

This one change has completely transformed how I frame and capture moments of gratitude. For example, when I ask: *"What am I thankful for?"* I write: *"My kids."*

When I ask: *"What do I want to remember, forever and ever, about yesterday?"* I write: *"I walked out of the house to find all three of my kids laughing and playing in the sprinklers and hoses on the trampoline in the summer sun. At ages 16, 13 and 8, those days of them playing together are few. I don't want to forget this."*

When I ask: *"What am I thankful for?"* I write: *"My husband."*

When I ask: *"What do I want to remember, forever and ever, about yesterday?"* I write: *"Last night Jon and I had a quiet dinner alone on the back porch. We enjoyed a glass of wine, and he told me all about a situation at work. I love when he opens up to me. We saw three baby deer come out of the woods, and we watched the yellow finches gather around the new birdfeeders he hung last weekend."*

I don't know why this one simple change caused such a profound difference in my attitude and my outlook, but it has. I still journal about the things that went poorly and strategize about how to improve them (that's how I grow), but I always begin by writing three things I want to remember forever and ever. Essentially, I'm saying to myself, *"Of all the mess and stress of yesterday, I'm choosing to remember these things instead."*

Here's an unexpected bonus: because I know tomorrow morning I'll be writing what I want to remember about today, it keeps me on the lookout for those things and makes me more aware of and more present with the beautiful, memorable moments in my life. Now, several times throughout my day, I say to myself, *"This is something I want to remember forever and ever—I'm writing about this tomorrow."* It causes me to pay better attention to the beautiful moments in my life.

It's impossible to be on the lookout for memorable moments and wallow in comparison at the same time. Since I started this practice, I have very little time, energy, or desire to look at anyone else (her home, her family, her body, her accomplishments) because I am too consumed with gratitude for the things God has entrusted to me.

"Let the peace of Christ rule in your hearts, since as members of one body you were called to peace. And be thankful." Colossians 3:15

"Rejoice always, pray continually, give thanks in all circumstances; for this is God's will for you in Christ Jesus." 1 Thessalonians 5:16-18

Gratitude is both the antidote to comparison and the highway to balance.

If you try nothing else from this list to free yourself from comparison, try this. I promise, it will change the way you *see* your life, which will then change your *actual* life.

What are three things you want to remember forever and ever about this lesson? (see what I did there?)

1. _____

2. _____

3. _____

Let's pray:

Lord,

Thank you for giving us the tools and strategies necessary for living a well-balanced life. I will use my powerful God-tools for smashing warped philosophies, for tearing down barriers erected against the truth of God, and for fitting every loose thought and emotion and impulse into the structure of life shaped by Christ. My tools are ready at hand for clearing the ground of every obstruction and building lives of obedience into maturity.

I will strip off and throw aside every unnecessary weight and sin which so readily, deftly and cleverly clings to and entangles me, and I will run with patient endurance and steady and active persistence the appointed course of the race that is set before me.

I will look away from all that distracts me, and look to Jesus. I will look straight ahead, not to the right or the left, or to any other person. I will fix my gaze directly before me. I will give careful thought to the paths of my feet and be steadfast in all my ways. I will keep my feet from evil.

When my eyes are healthy, my whole body is filled with light. So, I will set no worthless or wicked thing before my eyes. It will not grasp hold of me. Help me lay aside this yoke of oppression.

I will not speak maliciously about anyone. I will only speak words of life. Help me redirect my attention from the futile act of comparison to the spending myself on behalf of others: the needy, the hungry, and the oppressed. You promise when I do this, that my light will rise in the darkness and my night will become like day. Please guide me, satisfy my needs, and strengthen my frame. Make me a well-watered garden, like a spring whose waters never fail. Make me a woman of God who repairs, rebuilds, and restores.

Above all else, I will guard my heart, for everything flows from it. I will not be anxious about anything, but in every situation, by prayer and petition, with thanksgiving, I will present my requests to God. And the peace of God, which transcends all understanding, will guard my heart and mind in Christ Jesus. I will let the peace of Christ rule in my heart, for You have called me to a life of peace. Finally, I will pray continually and give thanks in all circumstances, for this is God's will for me in Christ Jesus.

In Jesus' name,

Amen

LESSON EIGHT

People Pleasing

My whole life, I've been surrounded by people who love me very much—people who care deeply about my decisions and their outcomes. People whom I admire and respect greatly: family, friends, and church leaders. I'm thankful for this. This was, and still is, a great thing.

Mostly.

I don't recall people pleasing being an issue for me as a child. Based on my memory, I would categorize myself as a strong-willed child. (I am now a self-proclaimed expert in diagnosing strong willed children, due solely to the fact that I have been blessed with one of my own.) I had strong opinions, and I wasn't afraid to share them. I had many friends, but like all kids, struggled to figure out who I was and where I fit. So, I did some dumb things out of peer pressure, for sure, but I wasn't a people pleaser...*yet.*

The seeds of people pleasing sprouted in the soil of my heart the year I graduated from high school.

The summer between graduation and college, I became very serious about my walk with God. I left the church I was raised in and was baptized into a new church. God radically changed the trajectory of my life that summer. A close family member was the assistant pastor of my new church, and several other family members attended there, as well. Everyone I knew at my new church was well-established, was very involved, and held leadership roles. So, from day one, I had access to the church leadership. I felt like the new kid at school who got invited to sit at the lunch table with the cool kids. I'm not gonna lie: It was pretty awesome.

As a new Christian, I could go to these people freely about anything and everything. I could sit in the pastor's office and chat through school struggles or relationship issues or questions about my faith, whenever I wanted! So, I did—all the time.

With wisdom and grace, they would patiently listen and then guide me in my decisions. What a blessing for a teen-aged girl who often had no clue about much of anything. They didn't seem to mind having me constantly come to them for advice, and I liked having access to their collective wisdom. I thanked God that He surrounded me with so many godly people who were interested in me and my new walk with the Lord.

I thought I was obeying God's word by seeking the counsel of many advisors. (Proverbs 15:22)

Over time, I started doubting my own ability to make sound decisions without first weighing them against the opinions of all these people— a.k.a. "The Committee" (not their real name, just what I call them in my head). The Committee then started sharing their opinions more often and more adamantly than I had requested. If I agreed with The Committee and took their advice, they were happy with me. I liked when they were happy with me. It felt good. If I expressed disagreement with The Committee, I would sense their disapproval, and I didn't like that at all. I felt like a little girl being chastised by her parents for misbehavior.

Because all of them were older, wiser, and godlier than me (I was not only a baby Christian, but also the baby of my family), I often deferred to them and their opinions, even if I didn't really want to, for fear of making poor decisions. I didn't like to be wrong (disagreement with them = wrong). But also, I didn't want to disappoint them. I wanted them to admire and respect me as much as I did them. I soon found out the way to achieve their admiration and respect was to go to them for every decision and then do what they'd said. This way, I always made sound decisions, and The Committee was always pleased with me. It was a win-win.

I thought I was following God's word by obeying those who had authority over me. (Hebrews 13:17)

Soon, I realized this was getting bigger than just me and The Committee. I didn't like the way it felt to disappoint *anyone*. Even if people barely knew me or had no concern for me or my future, I feared disappointing them. I didn't like the looks or the tones I'd receive when I had to tell people "no," even about small things. I didn't like to think I let people down in any way, so I said yes, a lot—I said yes to everything anyone asked me to, even when I didn't want to.

I thought I was obeying God's word by being a servant. (Matthew 20:26)

Over the years, I continued to say yes, and I was scared to tell people no. As a result, I became tired, stressed, conflicted, and resentful. By the time I had graduated from college—just four years later—I was a full-blown approval addict. I continued that way for the next decade.

I realized having so many people weighing in on my life's decisions posed another serious problem: they often didn't agree with one another. Inevitably, I was disappointing someone, somewhere, and I didn't like that at all. Worse yet, I had never really learned how to simply go to God and ask *Him* what I should do. Because The Committee was comprised of godly men and women—all of them pastors and ministry leaders—I assumed The Committee's opinion was also *God's opinion*. Sometimes, it was. Sometimes, it wasn't. I reached the point where I wasn't sure which was which, and the thought of disappointing God was almost more than I could bear.

So, one night at the age of 28, I stood in the back of my church, speaking with a man I loved and admired greatly—*my pastor*. At my side was another man I loved and admired greatly—*my husband*. We discussed one of the biggest decisions my husband and I would ever make—*a job change, a relocation 1,000 miles away, and a new church*.

The problem was these two men did not agree with one another. Symbolically, I had envisioned the hundreds of people who stood behind each of them, at odds with each other about what I should do. If I heeded the direction of my husband, I feared I would lose the respect and admiration of my pastor and the church family I had grown to love. If I heeded the direction of my pastor, I feared I could lose my marriage.

I wish I were exaggerating about the marriage thing, but I'm not. My new marriage was hanging by a thread for a lot of reasons–some big mistakes made in the first few months of our union, poor conflict strategies, and jobs that demanded too much of our time. At that point in our marriage, if I had dug in my heels and refused to support Jon in his new career opportunity, we would have divorced. I'm sure of it.

On the church and extended family side, I was entirely bound by fear due to years of dysfunctional reliance on other people and their ability to make decisions for me. I had no idea what a healthy boundary even was, let alone how to set one.

So, in one-life altering moment, as I stood between one man who had guided me through major life decisions since I was a teen and the other man to whom I had recently pledged my undying love, my respect, and my future, I heard myself utter these words:

"If I cannot hear the voice of God for myself, what hope do I have?"

That was 21 years ago. That night, I began my journey to learn to discern God's voice and break this dysfunctional cycle of people pleasing. It didn't break completely for many years, but I was on my way. I had no idea at that time how those words spoken in the back of a church in 1996 would shape my future. I had no idea that learning to hear the voice of God would be one of the most exciting and liberating experiences of my life. I had no idea how this one desire would grow into my life's passion and become material for multiple Bible studies, over a thousand blog posts, and the book you are holding. I had no idea how faithful God would be to speak directly to my heart, again and again and again. How that one moment would become the catalyst for teaching me to set healthy boundaries, so I could be completely free from people pleasing.

In the end, I decided to risk loss of reputation and respect of my church family and cling like crazy to my marriage. God met Jon and me there, guided us through the uncertainty, fear, and rejection and dumped a ton of grace and blessing into our lives. I knew I hurt some people in the process—a lot of them told us so—but God reassured us repeatedly it was most important to please *Him*.

Most women begin down the road of people pleasing with pure motives.

That was certainly true for me. We don't start by saying, "*I'm going to choose the will of other people over God's will for me.*" In fact, it's usually just the opposite. We start out thinking we are obeying God. We are trying to be nice, trying to serve, trying to keep peace.

Like any addiction, (drugs, alcohol, pornography, food) it grows little by little, decision by decision. The opinions of others become increasingly louder, deafening our ears to the whispers of God. Often by the time we realize what we are dealing with, we are so deep into it we don't know how to break free.

If you feel tired, stressed, conflicted, resentful, or unbalanced, people pleasing may be the culprit. In this lesson, we will look at some questions you can ask yourself to determine if this is a problem you need to address in your life. Then, in the next lesson, we will discover the path to freedom.

I promise, it is possible to break free. I'm living proof. After a decade of being entrenched in this bondage, I teach this lesson today from a position of complete freedom. I assure you, freedom from people pleasing, while a lot of hard work, is totally worth the effort.

Let's Define People Pleasing

I laid out an extreme people pleasing saga. Unlike me, few of us will be on the verge of divorce over it. Most of us who suffer from this condition exhibit it in more subtle ways. **Most people pleasers, for example, are known to be very "nice" and very "accessible."** They are the friends you go to when you need something: a ride, a dozen cookies for the bake sale, a hand with a home repair, a shoulder to cry on, a free baby sitter. Over-extending themselves is a way of life. It's how they roll. They are forever saying yes to request after request, with little regard to how it will affect them (or others) in the long run.

Just because you are nice or accessible doesn't mean you are a people pleaser, though. People pleasing has a unique component.

Les Carter, PhD, and author of the book *When Pleasing You is Killing Me* defines it this way, *"Unhealthy people pleasing is the tendency to cater to others' preferences to the detriment of personal well-being."*[20]

In other words, **people pleasers cater to others and their preferences until they, themselves, become emotionally, physically, relationally, and/or spiritually sick.**

Are you a people pleaser? Answer yes or no to the following questions. If yes, explain your answer.

1. Do you often feel responsible for the moods of others? Do you feel as if it is up to you to make sure everyone around you is happy? Do you feel guilty when they aren't?

For example, when you leave your spouse with the children, do you feel guilty when the children misbehave? Do you feel guilty because your spouse is stressed about the misbehavior? Do you feel responsible for all of it somehow—the behavior of the children and feelings of your spouse?

---

2. Do you sometimes find yourself being so generous with your time/effort/money/home that you encourage others to continue in irresponsible or disrespectful behavior? For example, do you cover for lazy co-workers, do all the housework, give money to your debt-ridden sibling, let your adult child live in your basement, eat your food, and play video games—all the while, seething as the person is taking advantage of you?

---

3. Do you have a difficult time telling people no, even to the detriment of your health or the health of your high-priority relationships? For example, do you take on more work than you can handle or continually work long hours because you fear what your employer will think if you don't? Do you agree to take on volunteering responsibilities that continually keep you away from your spouse and children, because saying no means people will think badly of you?

---

4. Do you find yourself constantly seeking approval or affirmation from other people for decisions you make—everything from where to live, to how to discipline your kids, to how to decorate your house? Do you rely heavily on feedback you receive through social media to make your decisions?

---

5. Do you find yourself bending over backward to get people to like you? Does it drive you crazy when you sense people don't like you, even if you don't really like them?

---

6. Do you find yourself continually committed to activities or responsibilities that you really don't want to do? Do you secretly feel resentment toward the people who asked you to commit?

People Pleasing vs. Biblical Servanthood

The most common question people ask me when I teach this lesson this: *"But since God calls me to be a servant, how do I know when I've crossed the line from servanthood into people pleasing?"*

The Bible is clear: not only does Jesus tell us to be servants of God and servants to each other, He modeled this way of life for us:

In your Bible, read Matthew 20:25-28. Write out verse 28 below:

But, being a people pleaser is different from being a servant of God. The apostle Paul draws that distinction in *Galatians 1:10. Read that verse in your Bible and fill in the blanks:*

"Am I now trying to win the _____ of men, or of God? Or am I trying to please men? If I were still trying to _____ _____ I would not be a _____ of _____."

So, where is the line between being a servant and trying to please men?

1. People pleasers feel trapped, but God's servants are free. People pleasers feel they have no choice in the matter. They become slaves to what other people expect of them or what they *think* other people expect of them. They may be serving well enough, but they are usually doing it reluctantly, from a place of bondage to the opinions of others. God, however, calls us to *freedom*. We are *free* to serve. **Biblical servanthood, therefore, is something that flows from our freedom in Christ.**

Underline the words "free" and "freedom" in Galatians 5:13-14 below:

13 You, my brothers and sisters, were called to be free. But do not use your freedom to indulge the flesh; rather, serve one another humbly in love. 14 For the entire law is fulfilled in keeping this one command: "Love your neighbor as yourself." Galatians 5:13-14

2. People pleasing is self-centered, but Biblical servanthood is others-centered. People pleasers reduce themselves to doing just about anything so people will think they are nice or smart. It's others-centered actions with self-centered motives.

It's *"I'm nice to you so you will like me."*

Biblical servants give of themselves because they love God and love others. It has nothing to do with how the person feels about her. Sure, a servant may receive the payoff of people's approval or gratefulness, but this is not the motivation behind the serving.

It's *"I'm nice to you because I love you."*

Look again at Galatians 5:13-14 above. Circle the word "love" wherever it appears.

From the outside, you may not be able to distinguish the people pleaser from the servant. The actions of the person who is operating out of freedom and love versus the actions of the person bound by people pleasing may look identical. The difference is the motivation behind the action or the root of the behavior.

The Root of People Pleasing

Fear

People pleasers are fearful people. Their motivation is not love. Sure, they may love the person they are trying to please, but their actions toward that person are not motivated by that love. Their actions are motivated by fear:

Fear of hurting someone's feelings.
Fear of abandonment.
Fear of someone else's anger.
Fear of punishment.
Fear of being shamed.
Fear of being seen as bad or selfish.
Fear of being or appearing to be unspiritual.

In your bible, read 1 John 4:7-18, and then answer the questions that follow:

1. Where does love come from? (vs 7)

_____

_____

2. What are we to do with this love? (vs 7 and vs 11)

_____

_____

_____

_____

_____

3. How many times does the word "love" appear in this passage? _____

4. Write out verse 18 word-for-word.

_____

_____

_____

_____

_____

5. Can love and fear co-exist? Why or why not?

_____

_____

_____

_____

_____

In context, this particular passage is talking about being sure of our salvation (that we will have confidence on the day of judgment). Love is the evidence of our salvation—our salvation is sure—which is why we will not be afraid or fear punishment after we die.

But this passage makes another truth abundantly clear: **God is love.** Not God *has* love, but God *is* love. We also know from Galatians 5:22 that love is a fruit of the Spirit. In other words, when we truly love others with the God-kind of love, this is evidence that God lives in us.

(Stick with me here. I'm going somewhere with this.)

People pleasers walk in fear. They treat people well because they are afraid of something. God's children walk in love. They treat people well because God is inside them, and therefore, *love is inside them.*

Now here's the beautiful thing: **Love is the antidote to all fear.** The perfect love that lives in you and causes you to serve others is also the love that drives out fear. God can and will drive out the root of fear that motivates your actions as a people pleaser.

Think about a particular person you have a difficult time refusing. What are you afraid of?

_____

Pride

Although people pleasers break their backs "doing" for other people, they are feasting solely on the payback of their approval. **People**

pleasers need people to focus on them, and they will go to exhausting lengths to have that need met. It is entirely self-serving.

Servants of God "do" for other people because they are focused on loving others, and ultimately want to point others to Christ.

Whenever we point the spotlight on ourselves (our efforts, our talents, our work) instead of God, it is pride.

In your Bible, read Proverbs 3:34, Proverbs 15:25, and Proverbs 16:5. Summarize in your own words how God feels about pride.

_____

_____

_____

Why People Pleasing is a Barrier to Balance

People pleasing and balance cannot co-exist. We are going to talk about why, but first, go back to Lesson 1 (page 22) and look at our definition of balance. Write it here, to refresh your memory, and then we'll discuss it:

_____

_____

_____

1. A well-balanced person is led by peace and lives a life marked by peace, but people pleasers are led by fear, guilt, frustration, and resentment.

God speaks to us through our conscience. He pokes and prods us along by His spirit to help us choose the path of righteousness. You know the uncomfortable "yuck" feeling you get when you do something wrong? That's God saying, *"Don't do that. That hurts Me. That hurts others. That will hurt you."*

God also gives you a good feeling inside (peace) when you do something right. That's God saying, *"Yes, do that. This pleases Me. This is what love looks like. This is good for you."*

A well-balanced person has a healthy relationship with her conscience and knows how to respond to it. Responding appropriately to the leading of God's spirit produces peace.

People pleasers, by contrast, have a faulty conscience. They lose the ability to discern God's disapproval from people's disapproval. This causes feelings of guilt and shame whenever they disappoint *anyone*, not just God. Their overly-critical conscience condemns them for things God Himself doesn't condemn them for. This causes unnecessary guilt, frustration, anger, and resentment.

Likewise, a people pleaser's faulty conscience blurs the distinction between the approval of people and the approval of God. It erroneously tells a person she is on the right track *when people are happy with her*—even if the action is in direct disobedience to God. This, of course, leads to a lack of true peace, because the people pleaser makes unwise decisions.

2. A well-balanced person knows her priorities. A people pleaser is unable to determine God's priorities for her. She becomes so concerned with what others think about her and becomes so accustomed to conforming her actions to meet everyone's expectations, she usually stops asking God what He thinks altogether. This dulls her sensitivity to God's spirit and her ability to discern His voice.

I remember as a newlywed, being unable to determine whether it was more important to stay late at work, go to (another) evening church function, or have dinner with my new husband, whom I had hardly seen all week. (Correct answer: GO HAVE DINNER WITH YOUR NEW HUSBAND, SANDY!) In those days, the loudest voice got the most attention. Since my husband was so quiet and the other voices were so loud, guess who ate dinner alone?

3. A well-balanced person lives her priorities. A people pleaser fails to live out her priorities, even if she knows what they are.

Instead, she starves her high-priority relationships of the time and attention they require because she is so busy fulfilling extra commitments.

At the height of my people pleasing days, I was a newlywed, working fifty hours a week (to please my boss and the hundreds of customers I serviced.), sang in three vocal groups at church (to please the music director, who was also a family member), and went to church four times a week (Wednesday night, Friday night, and twice on Sunday, to please all the church people—including my family.). Plus, I still tried to make time for my friends, my parents, and my other family members (we have a huge family). It was impossible for me to nurture my new marriage. Every yes I said to work, to church, or to other people was a no to Jon.

Remember: Every yes you say to someone costs you or the people you love something (time, energy, money, attention, focus.) If God leads you to a yes then the cost is irrelevant—God blesses this kind of yes, and He will redeem the time you give Him. However, if He did not tell you to do it, the cost can be more than your loved ones should pay.

If you resonate with this—if you feel a perpetual lack of peace because you can't discern your priorities, or you fail to live a life consistent with your priorities—I have great news: You can be free, but freedom may not be what you think it is.

What Freedom from People Pleasing is NOT

Whenever I teach on people pleasing, inevitably someone will shake her head and say, *"I'm not a people pleaser. I couldn't care less what people think of me."*

No, no, no. This is not freedom from people pleasing.

We *should* care what people think of us. I care very much what Jon and my kids think of me. I also care what you think of me. Why? Because I have a responsibility as a Christian to bear the image of Christ. My whole purpose on this earth is to know God and allow Him to conform my character to His character, so I can, then, extend His love to others.

Simply put: as I deal with others, I should be acting like Jesus.

I should be loving, patient, and kind. I shouldn't be self-seeking, proud, or boastful. If my boss is not "pleased" with me because I come in late, lie, cheat, steal, and act like a jerk—yeah, I better care about that. If I'm not portraying myself in a manner consistent with the image of Christ, and you call me out, I better care about that. If I hurt you, I must care about that.

In a way, I do want to please you. I want you to be happy with me. I don't live my life in total disregard for your opinion. However, freedom thrives in this type of "people pleasing," because my motivation for caring about what you think is *my love for God and my love for you.*

But if I'm loving God and loving you, and I do something that causes you to disapprove of me, I must transcend your opinion of me and obey God instead.

This is precisely what happens when I parent my children: They do something bad. I discipline them because I love God and love them. They hate me. I don't care.

Now if I go nutso on my kids while administering the discipline (hypothetically), and they bring it to my attention, I *should* care about this. **Being free from people pleasing does not mean we do whatever we want without regard to people.**

Read Galatians 5:13-26 in your Bible and answer the questions below.

1. *Write out the first sentence of verse 13.*

_____

_____

2. *Look at verses 13 and 14. What are the two behaviors contrasted here?*

"Indulging   in   _____   _____"   and   "serving   _____
_____ humbly in love."

3. *According to verses 16-18 and 24-25, how do we overcome our fleshly desires?*

_____

_____

4. *Look at verse 17. Explain why "freedom" is not the same as "doing whatever you want."*

_____

_____

5. *Look at the "acts of the flesh" in verses 19-21. List the ones that can involve behavior against or with other people.*

_____

_____

6. *Look at the "fruit of the Spirit" in verses 22-23. List the ones that can directly affect other people.*

_____

_____

As you can see, freedom is not doing whatever you want without regard to what others think or how it will affect them. It is actually the flesh that says, *"I don't care what people think. I'm going to do what I want."* The "*I don't care*" attitude is part of your flesh and is in direct conflict with the spirit of God. Freedom in Christ means loving people!

With that cleared up, I think it's time we break through this barrier. *Before we move on, don't forget to jot down a few things you learned in this lesson.*

1. _____

2. _____

3. _____

Let's pray:

Lord,

Thank you for showing me the difference between pleasing men and being Your servant. My heart's desire is to love You with my whole heart, mind, soul, and strength, and to love people as I love myself. Test my heart so that I love others in a way that pleases you, flowing from a heart that is filled with Your love. Though people may oppose my decisions, I pray for clarity to discern Your conviction when I have strayed from Your will and strength to walk in freedom. Let every decision I make be a decision rooted in love, not fear. Your perfect love casts out all fear.

As a woman approved by God to be entrusted with the gospel, I pray I will never put on a mask or use flattery or seek praise from men; but instead love others so deeply that I will be delighted to share with people not only the gospel, but my life as well.

In Jesus' name.

Amen.

LESSON NINE

People Pleasing, Continued

If it's true that my biggest area of personal growth has been in overcoming perfectionism, my growth in the area of people pleasing comes at a close second. It may even tie for first place. As I read through these personal anecdotes and examples, I hardly recognize that girl. Once bound by fear, frustration, and confusion, I now run my race with confidence. Once enslaved by the opinions and desires of others, I now live a well-balanced life marked by peace and freedom.

If you find your road to balance congested with misplaced guilt and resentment caused by people pleasing, this lesson will help you clear the way. Pick up your spiritual weapons, ladies, because it all begins with demolishing faulty mindsets.

Wrong mindset: I need everyone to like me.

Right mindset: Not everyone will like me or love me, and if they do, they shouldn't.

If everyone likes you, one of two things is probably true: either you are being dishonest with them by not portraying your true self, or they are being dishonest with you by not portraying their true feelings.

In your Bible, look up Luke 6:26 and write it, word for word.

———————————————————————————
———————————————————————————
———————————————————————————

Why do you think the people spoke well of the false prophets?

———————————————————————————
———————————————————————————

Wrong mindset: I need everyone to agree with or approve of the choices I make.

Right mindset: Someone will always disagree with my choices.

According to various Internet sources, we make about 35,000 decisions a day. With that number, it is impossible for every person we know to agree with each one. Even people who love us most and know us best will disagree with us for any number of reasons:

They don't have all the information.
They have a different perspective.
Something else worked better for them.
There is more than one right way to do something.

This is just life.

This is precisely why we must continually ask God for knowledge, wisdom, and understanding, so we make choices that are pleasing to Him.

In your Bible, read Colossians 1:9-10. What happens when God fills us with knowledge, wisdom, and understanding? (vs. 10)

———————————————————————————

Sometimes, people will disagree with our choices because they oppose our purpose or our mission. *In your Bible, read Acts 5:17-41 and then meet me back here to answer a few questions.*

1. *What did the angel of the Lord tell the apostles to do? (vs. 20)*

_____

_____

2. *What did the apostles do in response to this command? (vs. 21)*

_____

_____

3. *The apostles were brought in for questioning by the high priest before the Sanhedrin. What is the first thing Peter and the apostles said in response to them? (vs. 29)*

_____

_____

4. *After being persuaded by Gamaliel's speech, the Sanhedrin let the apostles go. Before they did, what happened? (vs. 40)*

_____

_____

5. *What did the apostles do in response to the flogging and the warning? (vv. 41-42)*

_____

_____

That is one of my favorite stories in the whole Bible. Even now, I have tears in my eyes as I marvel at the courage and joy the apostles exhibited in the face of persecution. We can learn a great deal from the apostles' response, especially if someone in our lives opposes the purposes of God and the clear direction He has given us. "We must obey God rather than human beings."

Is there anyone in your life right now who opposes your God-given purpose or mission? If so, how can you practically apply the concept of "We must obey God rather than human beings"?

Wrong Mindset: Everyone is judging me!

Right Mindset: People care less about what we do than we give them credit for.

After I moved to Florida, I remember worrying about what people *in Ohio* would think about certain decisions I was making—people I had not seen or spoken to in years. When Jon and I were choosing new friends, becoming established in our new jobs and new church, and making important financial decisions, I sometimes felt like "The Committee" was still in my head, opining about all the things I was doing wrong. I often had entire fake conversations with them, defending my choices. Yet, none of them was actually judging me at all—because most of them didn't even know what I was doing!

Even at the height of my people pleasing days, I projected my fear of rejection onto people who had neither a clue nor a care about my choices. In fact, I'm confident now that, given the opportunity to go back and appropriately limit my commitments at church and work, my boss and my church family would have been supportive. Sure, they would have been disappointed—maybe even upset at first—that I wouldn't be available to work longer hours or do whatever church thing I thought was so vital. But I know they cared much less than I assumed they did at the time.

In fact, when I finally stepped out and began setting healthy boundaries, the backlash was much less severe than what I had feared. Plus, my freedom to choose God's will over the will of people ultimately liberated others. As friends, coworkers, and family members, witnessed me taking a new stand—and doing so from a position of love for God and love for others—it freed them to do the same thing.

Think about the people you are trying to please. What is the **worst possible** *thing that will happen if you displease them? Is it possible that this is an exaggeration? Are you projecting your fear onto them unfairly, perhaps?*

Can you think of a person or people (someone under your influence who is also bound by people pleasing) who would directly benefit from your freedom from people pleasing?

Wrong Mindset: Jesus pleased everyone.

Right Mindset: Actually, He didn't.

Have you ever read through the gospels with an eye for how many times Jesus displeased people? Have you ever noticed how often He turned people away, didn't go when or where someone thought He should go, or didn't say what people thought He should say? If you find yourself dealing with rejection for your choices, you're in good company. _Take a look at these examples and answer the questions that follow:_

**Jesus disappoints his closest friends:** John 11: 1-6, 21

What did Mary and Martha want Jesus to do? (vs. 3)

What did Jesus do instead? (vs. 6)

How did Jesus feel about Mary, Martha, and Lazarus? (vv. 3 and 5)

**Jesus disappoints people under His leadership and teaching:** Mark 10: 17-22

What did the man want from Jesus? (vs. 17)

_____

_____

What did Jesus say to him that upset him? (vs. 21)

_____

_____

How did Jesus feel about this man? (vs. 21)

_____

_____

Jesus disappoints His family and religious leaders: Mark 3:20-22

What was Jesus doing in this scene? (vs. 20)

_____

_____

Describe how His family felt about this—what did they intend to do? (vs. 21)

_____

_____

Describe how the teachers of the law felt about this. (vs. 22)

_____

_____

Jesus disappoints the very people He was sent to save while doing good things: John 10:31-33 and Isaiah 53:2-3

What did Jesus do here that was so upsetting to the Jews? (John 10:33)

_____

_____

Write out Isaiah 53:3, word-for-word.

_____

_____

_____

Notice in each of the examples:

- Jesus was always acting out of love.
- He was always speaking truth.
- He was always in God's perfect will.
- He always lived a perfectly well-balanced life, being led by peace, knowing His priorities, and living His priorities.

And yet, He often displeased people. See? You're in good company.

Wrong Thinking: Saying no is bad.

Right Thinking: I need to say no to things I know I should not do.

About a year after we moved to Florida, I started having babies, and suddenly my priorities shifted. My children and my home became top priority, far above all outside commitments. As I was learning to set new boundaries around my time, my biggest stumbling block continued to be volunteer opportunities. Though I was often sleep-deprived, breast feeding, and working around nap schedules and diaper changes, it was difficult for me to refuse a friend who needed help. I'm not talking about emergencies...I'm talking about baking for the fund-raiser and organizing church picnics. It was especially hard if everyone else with babies (except me) was helping. I hated the thought that people might think poorly of me.

I remember asking my husband to help me practice saying no. He'd ask me a series of questions, pretending he was a friend who needed help with non-emergency type things. Sometimes, he'd use a high, feminine voice to make it super-realistic. **I practiced saying no politely, but firmly, without overly explaining myself.**

"That sounds like a wonderful event, but I won't be able to help you out with that. Thanks for understanding."

"Wow! You are doing some amazing things with this outreach! Unfortunately, we have a scheduling conflict and won't be able to attend."

And for people who wouldn't take no for an answer, I practiced saying this:

"Thanks for your opinion on that. You've given me something to think about."

These are all forms of the word "no."

If you are a people pleaser, learning to say no is like learning a foreign language. It's scary and uncomfortable. The first no is always the hardest. You'll fumble over your words, hesitate, and over-explain. You'll be tempted to retract and give in. This is why you must practice, practice, practice! It gets easier the more you do it.

As you say "no," remember these two things:

1. Don't be afraid of people:

In your Bible, look up Proverbs 29:25, and fill in the blanks:

"Fear of man will prove to be ___ _____, but whoever trusts in the Lord is kept _____."

2. Your goal is to please God:

"On the contrary, we speak as those approved by God to be entrusted with the gospel. We are not trying to please people but God, who tests our hearts."
1 Thessalonians 2:4

According to this verse, what is God testing?

_____

_____

Who is the hardest person or situation in your life to say "no" to?

_____

_____

Think of a word track (or borrow one from me!) that you can begin using today.

Wrong Mindset: I need to answer everyone immediately (which usually ends up being "yes.")

Right Mindset: I can delay my response.

As I mentioned previously, some people will not respect your "no." When this happens, it's common for recovering people pleasers to become confused. We start second-guessing our response. We wonder if our no should be yes. We can't tell if we are acting out of love or out of fear.

If someone is putting pressure on you to commit to something and you are not sure if it's God's will or just your old people pleasing ways creeping up, it's perfectly acceptable *to wait*. Delay your response. This gives you time to pray and/or get the courage to say no. Rarely, must decisions be made immediately. Emergencies aside, it's perfectly fine to take a few minutes/hours/days and think, pray, and ask a godly friend. Here are some of my favorite delay strategies:

"Can I get back to you on that? When do you need to know?"
"I need to check with my husband/my calendar before I can tell you for sure."

"If you need to know now, the answer will be no. But if you can wait, I'll think/pray about it and let you know later."

I can honestly say, these days, I almost never commit to something in the moment. I know myself well enough to know I always make better decisions about my time when I step away from the situation and think. Rarely have I (or the person asking) regretted taking a few hours or days to get clarity and perspective.

(We will also talk about this more in Lessons Ten and Eleven when we discuss busyness. As you may suspect, people pleasing and busyness can be closely related.)

What response can you give when you feel pressured to give an immediate answer?

Wrong Mindset: I am surrounded by controlling people—I have no choice but to give in.

Right Mindset: I have the power and the responsibility to distance myself (temporarily or permanently) from controlling relationships.

When we moved 1,000 miles from home, I put literal distance between myself and the people who controlled me. Maybe putting distance between you and the people who control you means you literally move away, too. Maybe you need to find a new church, a new job, or some new friends. Maybe it's time to block/unfriend/unfollow people on social media. Maybe it's time to give that adult child still living at home a 90-days eviction notice.

The magnitude of this step is not lost on me. I get it. Moving away from my hometown was the hardest thing I had ever done in my life, up to that point. However, the payoff (freedom from people pleasing, restoration of my marriage, and dependence on Jesus) was well worth the price.

Physical distance was good, but it wasn't enough. Even 20 years ago, people were only a phone call or email away. Therefore, it was equally important to put some emotional distance between us, as well.

First, I stopped asking advice from them. Maybe this sounds like a no-brainer, but it was counter-intuitive to me, mainly because I had depended on their advice for every decision I made for a solid decade.

Next, I stopped sharing the details of my life with them. This was huge. It turned out, they had nothing to disagree with once I stopped talking about my job, my church, my friends, my finances, my marriage, and my children. I didn't distance myself in this way from all people, though—only the ones who were controlling and opinionated. Honestly, I still refuse to share some things with certain people for this reason. I still have contact with them, but I've learned to deflect the conversation to talk about *them* instead of *me*. (P.S. People enjoy talking about themselves, so this works beautifully.)

Finally, I worked on establishing healthy boundaries around my home, my family, and my time. I decided the kind of life and family I wanted to have, and I protected the elements supporting this vision. This meant drawing firm boundaries around date night, family dinners, family vacations, and down time. It meant I was going to say no to many good things, even if I technically "had the time" to do them.

This is a process. It won't happen in a day. For me, it took a few years before I finally felt free. Take your time.

How can you put some distance between you and the people who tend to control you?

Wrong Mindset: I'm doing this all alone.

Right Mindset: I can choose a trusted friend to hold me accountable.

Accountability is an added layer of protection when you are learning how to say no and draw healthy boundaries. They will become a great sounding board during the *"can I get back to you on that"* period. For me, this person was (and still is) my husband. If your spouse is the person you are struggling to please all the time (in unhealthy ways) then choose someone else.

Look for someone who

- does not struggle with people pleasing
- has never attempted to control or manipulate you in the past
- has healthy relationships outside of yours
- will look at situations objectively
- will go to God on your behalf

If you don't know someone like this, ask God to show you someone. He will be faithful to bring godly people into your life. A good Christian counselor is also a wise choice, even if you have a godly friend or spouse.

Think of a trusted friend you can ask to hold you accountable. Name them here.

Two more words of wisdom I want to give you before we wrap up:

1. Keep your eyes looking straight ahead.

While I was recovering from a decade of people pleasing, I read Proverbs chapter 4, almost daily.

In your Bible, read the entire chapter of Proverbs 4—read it aloud, if you can, slowly and prayerfully. Jot down any verses or key words that stand out or thoughts you have while reading. Consider adding these things to the prayer at the end of this lesson to customize it just for you and your struggles.

2. Keep this word track handy.

When all is said and done—when you've gone through the process of changing unhealthy mindsets and responses, you've distanced yourself physically and emotionally from controlling people, and you've set new boundaries in place to protect your priorities—guess what?

There will still be some people who are not pleased with you!

It's true.

This is when it's time to speak two of the most liberating words in the English language: **Oh well!**

You can even do a little shoulder shrug with it.

Go ahead and practice: *"Oh well!"*

It's fun, isn't it? I say this often—to myself, or aloud—whenever I know I'm in the center of God's will and someone doesn't like what I'm doing. You don't need to be swept away emotionally every time someone gives you a disapproving look or tone. You don't need to flounder every time you disappoint someone. If you're walking with the Lord, seeking to do His will, loving God and loving your people, you don't need to second-guess every decision you make.

Girl, walk in confidence. Be comfortable in your skin. Be sure, whether people are on board with the direction you're headed or not, God's got your back. He is full of grace for the times you screw up—and you will screw up. It's okay. If you make a mistake and say "no" when it should be "yes" or say "yes" when it should be "no," don't worry. God will help you make it right and get you back on track to a life of balance. Either He will show you how to tactfully go back and change your response, or He'll use the mistake to teach you how to make better choices the next time.

Walking in peace. Knowing your priorities and living your priorities.

Your life and your time are too precious to wallow in bondage. Look at the barrier you just destroyed. It's crumbled at your feet. I'm so proud of you. It's time to step over it and continue running your race in freedom.

But wait! What are the three things that stood out to you in this lesson?

1. _____

2. _____

3. _____

Let's pray:

Lord,

I come to you today asking that you help me lay down the weight of people pleasing. Show me how to deal with others in a holy, righteous, and blameless way, as I encourage, comfort and urge them to live a life worthy of You.

Because I hear and follow the voice of the Good Shepherd, I refuse to follow the voice of a stranger. I listen closely to and pay attention to what You say to me. I do not let your words out of my sight, but keep them within my heart, for they are life to me and health to my whole body. I let my eyes look straight ahead, and fix my gaze directly before me. I make level paths for my feet and take only ways that are firm. I do not swerve to the right or to the left, and I keep my feet from evil.

Jesus, help me be more like You in all ways, especially the way You always did what was pleasing to the Father, despite the fact that many people disapproved of You, hated you, and ultimately crucified You. Help me seek approval from You, and You alone; for when I do, I will be completely free to hear your voice and love others the way You've commanded me to love.

In Jesus' name, I pray

Amen.

LESSON TEN

Busyness

"One of the great uses of Twitter and Facebook will be to prove at the Last Day that prayerlessness was not from lack of time"

John Piper [22]

Most of us *know* we are too busy. We admit it. We own it. We wear it like a badge of honor. When people ask us how we're doing, we don't respond with the traditional,

"Fine, thanks."

We say, *"Busy!"*

Or *"Fine. Busy."*

Or, my personal favorite *"Crazy-Busy!"*

"Busy" is the new "Fine."

Other than complete disconnection from God, nothing will hinder our ability to stay balanced more profoundly or more consistently than being overly busy. It's one of the enemy's most brilliant tactics. Over-commitment—*even with good, Christian things*—causes fatigue, resentment, bitterness, and ineffectiveness—*in all things.*

John Ortberg tells a story of a conversation he had with his mentor, Dallas Willard. As he describes it, his life was moving at a fast clip. He was, at the time, pastoring at one of the largest churches in the U.S.

while also parenting his young children through the "van-driving, soccer-league, piano-lesson, school-orientation-night years." (I feel you, John Ortberg.) In the midst of his hectic pace, Ortberg sensed his heart-condition suffering, so he sought counsel from his friend, *"What do I need to do to be spiritually healthy?"* he asked.

After Willard listened to Ortberg describe his plight, he paused and responded with, *"You must ruthlessly eliminate hurry from your life."*

Convinced this was the first of many units of spiritual wisdom on the subject, Ortberg agreed it was a good start, jotted it down, and waited to hear the rest of Willard's advice.

But Willard paused again, and said, *"There is nothing else. You must ruthlessly eliminate hurry from your life."*

Orberg concludes, *"… my life and the well-being of the people I serve depends on following his prescription, for hurry is the great enemy of spiritual life in our day. Hurry destroys souls."* [23]

Un-busy, un-hurried people are an anomaly. When we encounter them, we all stop and glare like we're viewing a rare exotic creature in a zoo exhibit. They are freaks, in the best sense of the word. In this lesson, we're going to discover how to become one of them.

Read Luke 10:38-42 and answer the questions below.

1. Look at verse 38. What exactly did Martha do?

_____

_____

2. Was this a "bad" thing? Circle the answer.

     Yes   *No*   *I'm not sure*

3. Look at verses 40 and 41. List all the adjectives used to describe Martha.

_____

_____

4. Look at verse 42. According to Jesus, how many things are actually needed?

_____

_____

5. What is this one thing?

_____

_____

I'm not gonna lie, I roll my eyes every time I open a women's Bible study and read about Mary and Martha (again!). Can we please leave poor Martha alone? I have such a soft spot in my heart for her. You guys, she invited Jesus (as in, *Jesus!*) and His disciples *into her home*. This was not something she had planned in advance. She didn't have time to prepare. This was a spontaneous invitation as Jesus and the disciples were passing through the town.

Be Martha for a minute. Picture yourself walking around your house in no make-up and sweats (or stirrup pants). You haven't picked up the mess from the night before. The toilets are a little gross. You haven't yet wiped the breakfast crumbs off the counter.

The next thing you know, a group of dirty, hungry men are following Jesus into your living room.

Martha was doing what any gracious and capable host would be doing—probably freaking out. I mean, probably fluffing pillows and tucking fresh blankets and sheets onto the beds, pouring beverages, and digging in her fridge to see what she could pull together for a meal. Maybe she was quickly throwing Lazarus' dirty underwear into a laundry basket and hiding it in her closet. In any case, she was trying to make her home comfortable for her guests. She was trying to love Jesus by extending hospitality.

None of this was bad.

But Martha can teach us a few things about busyness.

Busyness affects the heart. Jesus wasn't as concerned about Martha's actions as He was her attitude. Because Martha chose the "good" thing (making preparations for Jesus' stay) instead of the "better" thing (sitting at Jesus' feet and listening to Him), she became distracted, worried, and upset. Hurry is not just a disordered schedule. Hurry is a disordered heart.[24]

Loving people is difficult when we are hurried and rushed. When we become overwhelmed in our busyness, it's easy to look at the un-hurried, un-busy people and become irritated with them. Martha sees Mary *sitting* (the audacity!) at Jesus' feet, while she frantically tries to do everything herself. Instead of loving Mary, Martha is ticked off. I can relate. I get that way when I'm overscheduled, too. I look at people who are moving at a normal pace and think, *"Must be nice. I wish I had time for that."* Woe to the husband or child who is not helping me when company is coming. I get crabby. Then bossy. Then mean.

What happens to your attitude when you feel overly busy? How does it manifest in your interactions with others?

We cannot sustain an overly busy, hurried pace for the long-term without consequences. Eventually, it will affect us physically, emotionally, spiritually, and relationally. Perhaps you already understand the damage hurry leaves in its wake, but just in case you need further convincing, here are four more ways busyness negatively affects our balance:

Busyness makes us less productive and less effective. As women, we claim genetic rights to the ability to multitask. We boast about it, even. If we are talking on the phone, we are also folding a load of laundry. If we are checking math homework, we are also cooking dinner. If we are stuck in a meeting, a waiting room, or at a red light, we are catching up on emails.

I will confess to you right here right now, I stink at this. I cannot multitask. I once had a two-hour phone conversation with a long-winded friend and tried to redeem the time by unloading the dishwasher. I put away exactly 10 dishes. That's it. That's how much I stink. I stood at the dishwasher, holding a mug, unable to listen to my friend and also remember where the coffee mugs go.

I hate to break it to you, but you stink at it, too—you just may not realize it. Research shows most of us with normal human brains can't do multiple things at once, stay focused, and produce the same quality of work as we would if we simply did one thing at a time. A 2001 study[25] showed productivity to decrease up to 40% when we multitask. For companies, that translates to billions of dollars a year in lost revenue. For people like me, it means I'm burning dinner while checking math homework.

Busyness makes us sick. When we are too busy, we become stressed-out. Stress has extreme negative effects on our bodies, including headache, back pain, chest pain, heart palpitations, high blood pressure, decreased immunity, stomach upset, anxiety, depression, over-eating, and sleep disorders.[26] This alone makes me want to eliminate hurry from my life.

Busyness makes us unavailable to people. When I'm too busy, my relationships suffer. I don't have time to make a phone call or stop and talk for five minutes. Getting together with friends or helping someone in need is completely out of the question. When I'm crazy-busy, I avoid eye contact. I miss people entirely. I'm with my kids, but I don't see them. I'm spending time with them, except I'm not.

The Bible uses two words for time:

Chronos—meaning time in the way we measure it, with minutes, hours, and days.

Kairos—meaning "the appointed time" or "a time when conditions are right for the accomplishment of a crucial action: the opportune and decisive moment."

My pastor once said, "We often allow the routine of *chronos* to blind us to the opportunities of *kairos*."

This is what happened when Martha was so busy with preparations for Jesus that she missed the opportunity to sit at His feet and love her sister. This is what happens to me when I become so entrenched in the schedule of my day-to-day activities, I miss the opportunities God sets before me to connect with my people.

Read the following Bible passages where "kairos" is used and answer the questions that follow.

"15 Be very careful, then, how you live—not as unwise but as wise, 16 making the most of every opportunity (kairos), because the days are evil." Ephesians 5:15-16

"5 Be wise in the way you act toward outsiders; make the most of every opportunity (kairos). 6 Let your conversation be always full of grace, seasoned with salt, so that you may know how to answer everyone." Colossians 4:5-6

According to Ephesians 5:15 and Colossians 4:5, what do we need in order to "make the most of every opportunity/kairos"?

In your Bible, look up James 1:5. According to this verse, how do we get wisdom?

Busyness makes us unavailable to God. Connecting with God through prayer, worship, meditation, and Bible reading, require time (*chronos*). Literally, you need time to connect with God. Usually, when I am pressed for time, prayer and Bible reading are the first things to go.

Incidentally, it's this time (*chronos*) spent with God that yields the wisdom needed to discern opportunities (*kairos*) He presents to us. However, if I'm scheduled down to the minute with no margin in my day, how can I be available for *chronos* or *kairos* with God? I can't.

What problems do you see manifesting in your life right now as a result of your busyness?

_____

_____

Imagine yourself successfully eliminating hurry from your life. What does your life look like unhurried? What can you do now that you couldn't do before? Who are you connecting with? How is your health? Your rest? Your heart?

_____

_____

_____

_____

_____

What Kind of Busy Are You?

The reason I placed busyness as the final "Barrier to Balance" is because busyness is usually a secondary symptom of another root issue—usually one of the other barriers of perfectionism, comparison, and/or people pleasing—and they get all tangled up together. Without digging deeply, it's difficult to discern what caused what.

Just like an overweight person can also suffer from many other physical problems, like depression and joint trouble, it's difficult to know if the depression and joint trouble caused the excess weight or vice versa. Inevitably, they all feed on each other, causing a vicious negative health cycle: the person feels depressed and has joint pain, which make her less likely to exercise, which causes her to gain more weight, which exacerbates her depression and joint pain, etc.

The same thing happens here. Busyness is closely related to the comparison trap, perfectionism, and people pleasing that, at face value, you may have difficulty discerning what is causing what. They all exacerbate one another in a vicious downward spiral.

So, let's look at the different kinds of busy people to determine the root of your busyness. As you read through these descriptions, periodically rank yourself so you know where to direct your focus when it's time to eliminate hurry from your life. You will probably be a combination of a few of them.

The Poor Time Manager Busy Person

She feels unproductive in everything she does, and appears to be running around like the proverbial chicken with her head cut off. She does not have a problem with over commitment or too little time. Rather, she has a problem just managing the commitments and time she has.

Here is how she rolls: She gets up, starts her coffee and starts to unload the dishwasher. In the middle of unloading the dishwasher, she remembers she has wet clothes in the washing machine and goes to put them in the dryer. While she's in the laundry room, she sees a basket of clothes that need to go upstairs to the kids' rooms. She takes the basket upstairs and sees all the lights on and beds unmade. She makes beds, turns off lights, and grabs dirty cups from the bedrooms. On her way downstairs, she hears her phone ding. She checks her phone and responds to a text. That text reminds her she needs to write something on the calendar. She goes to write something on the calendar, and remembers she needs to confirm an appointment, she picks up her phone to make the call...

She is basically the main character in the children's book *If You Give a Pig a Pancake*.

Everything is always partially finished. At the end of her long, exhausting day, she looks around and asks, *"What in the world did I accomplish today?"* Her poor time management is probably a result of one of the following:

1. She doesn't know her priorities. She's not sure what's important and what is not, so she basically lets the loudest voice or the most urgent thing dictate her schedule. When the bills are due, she pays them. When the groceries run out, she shops. When someone needs help, she's there. Her lack of planning and ignorance of what's most important leads to frustration and spinning wheels.

This is not me at all			*This is sometimes me*					*This is me*	
1	*2*	*3*	*4*	*5*	*6*	*7*	*8*	*9*	*10*

2. She knows her priorities, but she doesn't know how to live them out. She knows she doesn't need a perfect house. She knows she doesn't have to cook gourmet meals each night. She knows it doesn't really matter if the upstairs bathroom is a mess or the laundry sits until she finishes unloading the dishwasher. She knows her family is her highest earthly priority. She knows she shouldn't stay on the phone for three hours or scroll through Pinterest until midnight, *but she has a hard time disciplining herself to live those things out.*

I need to insert a short rant here:

I originally wrote this lesson for a class I taught in 2009. Back then, I still had dial-up Internet. I did not have a smart phone. I had just joined Facebook. Pinterest and Instagram weren't "things" yet. In 2009, everyone I knew (including me) was busy, even without smart phones and Instagram. I wrote this lesson because *I needed this lesson.* I was too busy. Since that time, everyone (including me) has miraculously found additional hours in the day to spend glued to a screen.

I tend to pick on social media and blame it for everything bad in the world. While this may be unfair to pick on social media, we cannot deny that technology is a huge contributor to busyness and hurry. We cannot have a discussion about busyness and balance without addressing it. Consider:

- It's a time sucker—the average person spends about two hours a day on social media[27] and touches her phone 2,617 times a day![28]

- It puts us on information overload—pumping into our brains a steady stream of news, trivia, and advertisements, 24-hours a day.
- It distracts us from completing any task requiring focus.

Thus, a person in this category finds herself sucked into the smart phone vortex for an hour (or three) while her priorities and obligations take a back seat. Then at the end of the day, she beats herself up for wasting time, vowing to do better tomorrow, but the cycle repeats itself, day after day.

This is not me at all				*This is sometimes me*				*This is me*	
1	2	3	4	5	6	7	8	9	10

3. She is a perfectionist. She knows her priorities and she attempts to live them out, but she spends too much time doing each activity just right. She prioritizes well enough, but always finds herself stuck in the rut of details. We covered this in Lessons Four and Five, where we firmly established perfectionism as a time-sucker. If this is your issue, you know who you are.

This is not me at all				*This is sometimes me*				*This is me*	
1	2	3	4	5	6	7	8	9	10

The Over-Committed Busy Person

She truly has too much on her plate. She tries to defy laws of nature by taking on more than is humanly possible and cramming too much into life. She often sacrifices prayer, sleep, and recreation to accomplish all she's committed to. She's probably this way for one of the following reasons:

1. She's a people pleaser. She doesn't know how to say no, or she's afraid to say no. She likes the affirmation she receives when she steps in and takes over. She doesn't want to disappoint anyone, so she says yes to everything. We covered this in Lessons Eight and Nine—all the people pleasers, please step forward.

This is not me at all   *This is sometimes me*   *This is me*
1   2   3   4   5   6   7   8   9   10

2. She feels trapped and believes she has no control over her schedule. Between her job, her spouse's job, her kids' activities, and all her volunteer commitments, she sincerely cannot see any place to cut one thing back. If you were to guide her through each item on her schedule, she would defend each thing and explain why it is vital to her existence and to the existence of all mankind.

This is not me at all   *This is sometimes me*   *This is me*
1   2   3   4   5   6   7   8   9   10

3. She's trapped by comparison. She tries to keep up with what everyone else is doing, because doing these things makes her feel important or worthy. She derives her value from her accomplishments because, when she does certain things, she measures up to her peers. Therefore, she commits to a lot of things she cannot or should not be doing. Since we covered Comparison in Lessons Six and Seven, this should sound familiar to all who struggle with this.

This is not me at all   *This is sometimes me*   *This is me*
1   2   3   4   5   6   7   8   9   10

4. She doesn't see the value of a non-busy life. She would tell you she has a strong work ethic. Time is money, after all. She is critical of those who move slowly. To her it comes down to simple math: Busy=Productive=Important=Godly.
Un-busy= Unproductive=Lazy=Ungodly.

She has an insatiable inner drive that pushes her far past her limits, often to her own detriment. She loves living at a fast pace and ends up dragging her kids along as she races from thing to thing. Her most-used phrase is "Hurry up." That is, until her body starts to crumble from the constant pressure: she falls ill, or can't sleep, or finds herself in the ER with heart palpitations. She is as surprised as anyone to discover she's not Wonder Woman. In fact, she may not be fully convinced of this discovery, even in the midst of a health scare.

This is not me at all			*This is sometimes me*					*This is me*	
1	*2*	*3*	*4*	*5*	*6*	*7*	*8*	*9*	*10*

Write the area(s) where you ranked yourself 4 to 7:

_____

_____

Write the area(s) where you ranked yourself 8 to 10:

_____

_____

In summary, what appears to be your primary issue(s) that lead(s) to your busyness?

_____

_____

In the next lesson we are going to begin the destruction of this barrier, but before we do, here are a few things to keep in mind:

First, remember our lesson on people pleasing, where we said the Biblical response to people pleasing is not *"I couldn't care less what people think about me"*? In the same way, the Biblical response to busyness is not *"Well, then, I'll do the opposite of busy—which is nothing. I will do absolutely nothing."*

Getting "un-busy" or living an "un-hurried" life does not mean we neglect work. Work is good. We are all called to work to provide for our families, to provide for ourselves, to be good stewards of the material goods God has given us, to serve others, and to use our gifts and talents to edify the Body of Christ. So, if you think the answer to your hurried, busy life is to lie around and collect unemployment, while your laundry and dishes pile up and your kids run around undisciplined, think again. That isn't God's will for you either.

Second, getting "un-busy" is hard work. If it were as easy as cancelling a few non-essential events or crossing a few items off our to-do lists, wouldn't we have done that already? For most of us, it's actually quite complicated. Our lives are intertwined with the lives of our spouses, our children, our extended family and friends, as well as the agendas of our employers, our churches, and a host of other organizations who (unfortunately) cannot set their schedules based upon our priorities. Our best intentions at living out our priorities can be thwarted by sickness, weather, babysitter cancellation, or mechanical breakdown of automobile and/or major appliance. You may be fighting against a corporate culture, a church environment, or family dynamic that is bigger than you.

Third, getting "un-busy" requires constant maintenance. This is not a "one and done" situation. Think of your life like a garden. Left unattended, even a flourishing garden will eventually become overrun with weeds and pests. To remain fruitful, a garden requires regular watering, weeding, uprooting, replanting, pruning, and harvesting. This doesn't mean something's wrong with the garden. It means it's alive.

Fourth, even if you and I had the exact same number of things on our agenda, one of us could feel very hurried and one of us could not. We are all made differently. We all have a different "busyness threshold". So, don't look around at what anyone else is doing or refraining from doing. Just keep your eyes on your own schedule during this exercise.

Finally, your root issue will determine your remedy. How you ranked yourself in the descriptions of different kinds of busy people will determine how you proceed.

In the next lesson, we will hit this from every angle. Some of the suggestions and action steps may not apply to you at all—go ahead and skip those. Some of them will be exactly what you need—focus your efforts here. Only you know you. If you are not sure if something applies, pray and ask God to give you wisdom about your busy-hurried heart.

By the way, you may want to grab your calendar for this next lesson, because we're about to rearrange it.

First, I need you to quickly jot down three things you learned in this lesson:

1. _____

2. _____

3. _____

Let's pray:

Lord,

I feel worried and upset about many things. You said only one thing is needed: to sit at your feet and listen to you speak. So, today I come to you and ask, what would bring You glory? Where should I focus my attention? What is the best use of my time? Please speak to me.

Help me, Lord, to live out my priorities—loving God and loving people. Nothing more, nothing less.

I know anxiety does not come from You. You are Peace, and You desire for me to live in Peace. So, I will not be anxious about anything, but in every situation, by prayer and petition, with thanksgiving, present my requests to God. And the peace of God, which transcends all understanding, will guard my heart and my mind in Christ Jesus.

I will not worry about my life. I will stop being preoccupied with getting so I can respond to Your giving. I do not want to be like those who do not know You. I want to steep myself in Your reality, Your initiatives, and Your provisions. I will not worry about missing out.

In You, I find that all my everyday human concerns will be met. I will give my entire attention to what You are doing right now. I will not get worked up about what may or may not happen tomorrow. I know You will help me deal with whatever hard thing comes up when the time comes.

In Jesus' name.

Amen.

LESSON ELEVEN

Busyness, Continued

"It wasn't just the sheer number of things that felt overwhelming, it was the familiar stress of many tasks vying for top billing at the same time."

Greg McKeown [29]

A few years ago, I reached a crisis point. Honestly, I didn't see it coming. Everything on my calendar was "good" stuff. I still had a preschooler at home, and the two older kids were in multiple after school activities. This meant dinner on the go and late bed times. Jon was climbing the corporate ladder, which meant early mornings and late nights for him (and me).

My days were so full, I had absolutely no margin. I was exhausted all the time. I was irritable and short-tempered with my kids. I was forgetting important things—like paying bills and showing up at the right place and time to pick up kids. I had little joy and little peace. I just kept slapping a smile on my face as I loaded everyone into the car for the next event.

In a desperate attempt to gain some balance, I quit everything. Literally. As each sports season ended, I told the kids *"No activities…none. Don't even ask."* I informed my church small-group leader we'd be taking a hiatus from our weekly meetings. (A hiatus that has lasted nine years and counting.) I stepped down from my ministry commitments at church—*all of them.* I discontinued the Bible study I taught in my home.

I was ruthless. (Dallas Willard would have been so proud.)

For several months, our family did nothing beyond school, homework, eating, and unstructured recreation. This break gave me the much-needed rest and clarity to discern which activities were vital and which ones were not. Eventually, I added some things back into my schedule, but this time, I did it with great intention, careful to leave plenty of margin so I wouldn't end up in the same sinking boat. (Incidentally, this was also the same time I wrote the first draft of this Bible lesson on busyness!)

If you are there, and you feel your little boat sinking, you may not need such a radical approach, but you must take action. In this lesson, I will lead you through a process to determine what stays in your boat and what gets thrown overboard. This lesson is very hands-on, so prepare yourself for some work. Also, I wasn't kidding about grabbing your calendar—you'll need it.

Breaking Through the Barrier of Busyness

1. Go on a fast. I know. What a horrible first step. No one likes fasting. Fasting is hard. You're going to be tempted to believe this step doesn't apply to you. Don't skip it though. This one is for everybody. The act of denying your self-centered flesh what it desires and instead feeding your soul with God's word is a perfect environment to hear God speak. If you're serious about eliminating hurry, I recommend you begin here—that means *all y'all*. Take a day, a week, or longer for the sole purpose of fasting and hearing God about your overly busy life.

I mentioned earlier that every January, I go on a month-long partial fast to prepare my heart for the upcoming year. I pray over all my commitments and responsibilities, and I ask God for wisdom so I don't overcommit. I also take shorter fasts throughout the year. I'm on one now as I write this. It is a sober reminder that my time is not my own.

If you are unfamiliar with Biblical fasting, here are a few scriptures to guide you. As you read, jot down notes or anything that jumps out at you:

Daniel 10

_____

_____

Isaiah 58

_____

_____

Ezra 8:21-23

_____

_____

Joel 2:12-13

_____

_____

Matthew 6:6-18

_____

_____

Acts 13:1-4

_____

_____

Action Step: Have you ever been a fast? Set aside a day in the next two weeks to fast and pray about your busy schedule. Write the date of your fast here and also add them to your calendar:

_____

_____

2. Remember your priorities. We've been talking about our priorities since the first lesson. *Read Matthew 22:37-40 from The Message below to refresh your memory about your top priorities:*

"Jesus said, "'Love the Lord your God with all your passion and prayer and intelligence.' This is the most important, the first on any list. But there is a second to

set alongside it: 'Love others as well as you love yourself.' These two commands are pegs; everything in God's Law and the Prophets hangs from them."

The command to love God and love others plays out differently for each person and in each season of life. As a new Christian and a young wife, I was often confused about my priorities. I knew I should love God and love others, but I didn't know what that looked like practically. This caused me to over-schedule and over-commit repeatedly, often to the detriment of my marriage and my health. Once I understood, Biblically, how to prioritize my various responsibilities and relationships, I was able to prioritize my schedule to reflect that.

The following are the major items most women need to prioritize. Place a check mark next to or highlight the ones that apply to you:

- **God**: This includes prayer, worship, Bible reading, seeking His will and direction for your life, listening for His voice, and allowing Him to conform you to His image.

- **Your Spiritual Growth:** This is not your daily time with God, but rather, the additional things you do to enhance your walk with God. This may include church attendance, small group participation, group Bible studies, reading spiritually uplifting books, and attending retreats and conferences.

- **Your Physical Well-Being:** This includes a healthy diet, adequate daily/nightly rest, and regular exercise.

- **Your home:** This is not only maintaining your house, but also creating a peaceful and nurturing environment for your family and friends.

- **Your Job:** This includes any paid or unpaid jobs outside the home or from the home, part-time or full-time.

- **Your Ministry Activities:** These are things you do where you use your gifts and talents to be an active part of the Body of

Christ. Maybe you sing in the choir, teach classes, volunteer as a greeter, or serve the homeless. Name the ways you serve here:

- **Your Marriage:** If you are married, write the name of your spouse here:

- **Your Children:** If you have children, write the names and ages of your children here:

- **Your boyfriend or fiancé:** Write his name here:

- **Extended family:** This includes your parents, in-laws, your siblings and their families, grandparents, aunts and uncles, cousins, etc. Briefly describe your relationship with your extended family (for example, if they live out of town or in your home). This will help you determine where they should fall on your list of priorities.

- **Friends:** You may rank your "inner circle friends" a higher priority than the rest of your friends. Name your closest friends here:

- **Other activities:** These are recreational things you do that keep you balanced. This may include reading fiction, refinishing old furniture, photography, taking your kids to the pool, going to the theater, hiking, or cooking for fun. Whatever you do that makes you come alive, make room for it in your schedule. Name these things here:

- **Other:** Did I miss anything important to you? Name it here:

Before you rank them, keep these things in mind:

- Your list of priorities is a nice guideline, but in the event of an emergency, this list gets thrown out the window. Ditto, if God speaks to your heart and tells you to tend to things out of order for a day or for a season. For example, when I received a call from my sister telling me my dad, who lives five hours away, was critically ill, I left as quickly as I could. At this stage of my life, as a married woman with three children in my home, my dad is normally low on my list of daily priorities, but on that day, he shot up to number one. I cancelled all my commitments, left my children (high priority) with my husband (high priority), and packed a suitcase for several days where I sat by his bedside.

- Many items on this list overlap, so tending to one is usually not at the exclusion of all others. For example, on my list of priorities, I rank "friends" pretty low—which makes it look like I don't care about my friends. Then again, many other high priorities directly involve my friends. When I worked outside the home (a high priority), my best friends were my co-workers. I saw them every day. We talked, ate lunch, and often socialized regularly. When I was a mom to toddlers and preschoolers (a high priority), I interacted daily with other moms at the park and in the neighborhood while our children played together. Now, teaching (which shows up as high priorities in both "my job" and "my ministry") involves spending several hours every week with my very best friends.

- If you have small children, most of your high priorities will merge together on most days (spending time with your husband and your children at the same time, praying and taking care of kids at the same time, exercising and taking care of kids at the same time, grocery shopping and taking care of kids at the same time...)

- Contrary to popular belief, the time you devote to your tasks is not always indicative of the place it holds on your priority list. I know, for example, that I'm more important to Jon than his job. However, he most often spends more of his waking hours at work than he does alone with me.

- This list is a work in progress. It has taken me years of seeking God and lots of trial and error to develop my list of priorities. I revisit it and adjust it often—always annually and often seasonally. I suggest you use this as a template. As various opportunities present themselves, this tool will help you say yes and no to the correct things in an effort to sustain an unhurried pace. Remember, it's fluid, not set in concrete.

Action Step: Prayerfully rank your priorities here, as best you can. (I recommend you use pencil—you probably won't get it right the first time.) This will be your guide when determining what is added or eliminated from your schedule.

1.

2.

3.

4.

5.

6.

7.

8.

9.

10.

11.

12.

13.

14.

15.

3. Know your gifts and talents: Operating primarily in the areas where I am gifted has freed up my schedule more than almost anything else.[30] When I was in my 20s and early 30s, I felt obligated to fill every gap and tend to every need presented to me. Because I could adequately perform many tasks, I thought I was mandated by God to do so. My motto was, *"If I can do it, I should do it."* Consequently, I said yes to almost everything. This, obviously, led to confusion and chaos in my schedule.

But as I spent more time getting to know God (my highest priority), He began revealing to me His specific purposes for me. This insight helped me know where to focus my time, and just as importantly, helped me to know where *not* to focus my time. It gave me the freedom to say no to everything outside of my specific purpose.

For example, writing and teaching are my primary gifts. This is why, with a very clear conscience, I spend more than 20 hours a week writing and teaching and say no to almost every volunteer opportunity.

Read 1 Corinthians 12:4-31 and answer the questions below:

   1. Who determines what spiritual gifts we have? (vv. 4-6, 11)

_____

_____

   2. Why do we have spiritual gifts? (Vs. 7)

_____

_____

3. Look at verses 17-20. Explain in your own words why it's important that you operate in your unique gifts and not try to be like someone else.

Action Step: What is something you are especially good at that you also enjoy? (You may be good at something, but hate it—for me, that's being Room Mom. Or you may love something and not be very good at it—think bad American Idol auditions.) The point where your talents and your passions intersect is usually a big, giant arrow pointing to your spiritual gift.)

How can you use this gift for the common good of the Body of Christ?

Do you have any current commitments that you know for certain do not fall in alignment with your spiritual gifts? Is there something you can get off your schedule today? Write it here, and then make arrangements to remove that thing from your plate, find your replacement, or give your notice.

---

4. Understand your season: When I was a new mom, well-meaning older women often said, *"Remember, your husband is still your top priority."* This confused and frustrated me. I'd look down at my five-pound preemie and think, *"How is it that this tiny baby is not my top priority? If I don't feed my baby, he'll die. If I don't feed Jon, he'll walk into the kitchen and make a sandwich."*

Right?!

Then, one day when I was seeking clarification from a trusted friend, she lovingly reminded me about seasons. She assured me that my babies would only be babies for a little while. While it was true that my marriage was usually my top earthly priority, it was also essential that I spend a disproportionate amount of time caring for my babies *for a season*. God designed it that way. Babies are absolutely helpless. I didn't need to feel a moment of guilt for taking the majority of my days caring for the babies. As the season changed, so did my distribution of time and attention, and I'm happy to report, no one starved.

Read Daniel 2:21 and write it word for word here:

_____

_____

_____

_____

While I write this, my windows are wide open. Spring is here and the weather is perfect. A few short weeks ago, however, I was sitting next to the fire wrapped in a blanket—*looking at snow*. With seasonal weather changes, we participate in activities unique to each season. Consider what would happen, for example, if in January we ignored the sub-zero temperatures and six inches of snow, and insisted on wearing tank tops and flip-flops? Or what if in July we ignored the heat and humidity, closed up our car and left the dog in there? We must realign our behavior based on the season. To ignore these is both unwise and dangerous.

Look up Ecclesiastes 3:1 and fill in the blanks:

"There is ____ _____ for everything, and a _____ for every activity under the heavens."

The same is true for seasons of life. Having babies was one unique season requiring a temporary realignment of priorities. Had I not done this, I would have put my baby in danger.

Here are a few other distinct life seasons I have encountered requiring temporary realignment of priorities:

- Seasons of grief, where I did little more than exist

- Seasons of change, where I spent time laying foundations and establishing roots in a new city (twice)

- Seasons of growth, where I spent an exorbitant amount of time reading and studying, laying a foundation for future ministry

- Seasons of healing, where I spent months in counseling for clinical depression

- Seasons of ministry, where I spent months preparing for and teaching Bible studies

- Seasons of intense, hands-on parenting, as my kids struggled through some challenges in their lives

Identifying your season will liberate you to focus on certain things temporarily without confusion or guilt. If you are trying to get out of debt, then cooking meals at home, cutting coupons, and taking extra jobs will be your priority. If you are taking control of your health, then eating healthy meals and daily exercise will be your priority. If you are caring for aging parents, then hiring someone to clean your own house may be a priority. If you are working on your marriage, then counseling and date nights may be a priority.

Action Step: Identify your season. What adjustments should you make for a period of time to reflect the priorities unique to this season.

---

5. Understand the Full Extent of a Commitment Before You Commit.

Read Luke 14: 28-32 and answer the question below.

According to verses 29-30 and 32, what are the consequences of moving forward without first estimating the cost?"

Jesus understood the need to consider the full cost—in money, time, and resources—before diving in to something new. I've never personally built a tower or gone to war, so let's consider a more relevant example: Dance lessons. Let's pretend your daughter wants to sign up for a one-hour dance class. The lesson is held each Wednesday from 5:00 p.m. to 6:00 p.m. That's one hour a week, right?

Wrong.

Don't forget to add time for driving in rush hour traffic.

Remember children move more slowly than adults do. They also lose shoes and need snacks. Depending on the age of your child, you may need to build in a cushion for "kid time."

A 5:00 p.m. dance lesson takes place over the dinner hour. That means either you must plan an easy dinner on Wednesdays or cook something ahead of time—otherwise you're eating at 8:00 p.m., or blowing the budget (and your diet) in the drive-thru.

Do you have other kids? Will you need to take other kids with you or arrange for childcare?

What about homework? Will you need to rush through homework before lessons or after dinner?

Don't forget the dance recital (or three!), which also means additional money and time.

Oh, and you need leotards and tights. And also, two pairs of shoes (ballet and tap). Add "shopping" to your calendar and your budget.

Clearly, it's more than a one-hour dance lesson! As you consider taking on new commitments, dissect them and count the true cost—both for your finances and your calendar.

Action Step: Are you currently committed to an activity or considering a commitment that may be more than you can handle? Write out every detail of the time required here. Then prayerfully consider if this is a good use of your time:

_____
_____
_____
_____
_____

6. Get help. Sometimes scripture is cryptic and difficult to apply to life. And sometimes it's *this*. If ever a story exists that gives us permission to get things off our plate and get help, this is it.

Read Exodus 18:1-27 and answer the questions below:

What was Moses doing every day? (vv. 13-14)

_____
_____

Write verses 17 and 18 word-for-word. Why is it important to delegate?

_____
_____

What did Jethro suggest Moses do instead? Summarize it in your own words? (vv. 19-22)

_____
_____
_____
_____

What would be the result, if Moses took Jethro's advice? (vs. 23)

Sometimes we do important work we are simply not meant to do alone. When I had my first office job, my boss gave me some excellent advice, *"Figure out what only you can do, and then delegate everything else."* I've continued to apply that advice to my life, even 25 years later.

Truly, some things only *you* can do, but those things are fewer than you think. Depending on your current level of hurry, everything else should be delegated. In other words, it's perfectly okay to enlist help with your daily tasks.

Let me lift a load off you right now: unless you love cleaning your own house or you truly cannot afford it, it's okay to hire a cleaning lady—even if it's only once to get your house spotless from top to bottom.

Hire a teen to cut your lawn. (Teens need money. In fact, please hire my teen.)

Delegate chores to your children—kids are cheap labor, plus you're teaching them essential life-skills.

Hire a babysitter, or ask your 12-year-old neighbor to be your helper after school.

Find like-minded moms to swap childcare with you.

Take your clothes to the cleaners.

Order pizza.

Asking for help, delegating, hiring people to do time-consuming chores—these are all good things! By doing so, you will add hours back into your week.

Action Step: Look at your daily and weekly tasks. Write them all out on the blank page at the end of this book. From that list, identify the things that only you can do. (Hint: These should be a short list. It should include specific "wife duties" that would be immoral for someone else to perform {ahem}, certain childcare duties like loving and teaching your kids morals, and specific job functions that are integral to your position.) Everything else is up for discussion. Start looking for ways to delegate or get help with "everything else."

7. Simplify.

When our family moved into our current house, I purged our home of about 50% of our possessions. Our home had never been overly cluttered—or so I thought. I figured it would take me a couple days and a trip or two to Goodwill.

Hahahahaha. *Oh, Sandy, you are so adorable when you are naïve.*

I dubbed my simplification project, "Operation Spring Clean: No Drawer Left Behind."

Over the course of a few months (not days), I gave away or sold multiple items of furniture. I rid my closet of every item of clothing I did not absolutely love. I forced my kids to choose only their most cherished toys. I even purged our storage and garage of crap (yes, most of it was crap) we had accumulated over two decades of marriage and 18 years of parenting.

I drove my packed SUV full of donations to Goodwill at least 20 times. It was a lot of hard work. But the clarity and freedom I have experienced from reducing the clutter in my home is remarkable.

Read Luke 12: 13-48 in your Bible, and then meet me back here.

Jesus spends the majority of this chapter warning us against the lure of material possessions. He urges us instead, to trust God to supply our needs and focus our attention on eternal life.

Then, He makes this statement in *Luke 12:48: "When someone has been given much, much will be required in return; and when someone has been entrusted with much, even more will be required."*

From a very practical standpoint, having a lot of stuff means having a lot of stuff to care for.

After the initial investment of time, sorting, selling, and donating our material possessions, I've spent the last two years reaping the benefits. The act of simplifying our stuff brought clarity in both my mind and my schedule in ways that continue even to this day. Now, my house usually looks presentable. (I say usually because we still have five people living here. This isn't the Pottery Barn catalogue.) When it gets messy, I can straighten it in no time. Since I've purged my closets, drawers, and cabinets, I have space to store all our things—I even have some empty shelves and cabinets. This means I spend less time cleaning, less time organizing, and less time trying to find things. Because I've streamlined my wardrobe, I spend less time trying to decide what to wear.

All this means less stress and more time to do other things—or do nothing at all.

Read this passage and answer the questions that follow:

"I do want to point out, friends, that time is of the essence. There is no time to waste, so don't complicate your lives unnecessarily. Keep it simple—in marriage, grief, joy, whatever. Even in ordinary things—your daily routines of shopping, and so on. Deal as sparingly as possible with the things the world thrusts on you. This world as you see it is on its way out." 1 Corinthians 7:29-31 (MSG)

1. According to this passage, what is the actual source of your complicated life— who or what is thrusting things on you? (Circle the correct answer)

      My sinful nature   *Satan*   *The world*

2. This passage identifies three reasons we should seek simplicity. Fill in the blanks.

- *Time is _____ _____ _____.*
- *There is no _____ to waste.*
- *The _____ as you see it is on its way out.*

3. In your Bible, look up 1 Corinthians 2:12 and write it here:

_____

_____

_____

Action Step: What is one area of your life you know you should simplify? Is it a room in your house? A routine? A chore?

_____

_____

Simplify something. Start somewhere easy to help give you momentum (Your car's glove compartment. What you eat for breakfast. After dinner clean up). Devote just 30 minutes to simplifying this area of your life. Write the date and the area you're simplifying here:

_____

_____

8. Set Annual, Monthly, and Daily Goals. The main reason I go on an extended fast each January is to seek God in setting goals for the upcoming year. Setting goals helps me distribute my time each day. When I set goals, I usually look at the main areas of my life: spiritual, ministry, work, family, and health. I don't always have goals in every area, but this helps me narrow down some areas where I want to grow, learn, or excel. For example, this year one of my annual goals is to write, publish, and launch this Bible Study.

At the beginning of each month, I look back at those goals, and I take some time to ask God for direction about them. I ask, *"Is this still a viable goal? Has the goal shifted or changed?'* If it's still an area of priority, I try to set a mini-monthly goal for each major goal—something I can do to support the bigger annual goal. For one mini-goal this month, I'm trying to complete this lesson and do a final read-through of the entire study.

Then, each night before bed, I take a few moments to jot down three or four things I want to accomplish the next day that support the monthly goal. This is not overkill. It requires no fancy planners (unless you like fancy planners). Literally, I take loose-leaf paper in a three-ring binder and write a few things down: something to support the monthly goal (Today, it's writing for two hours), what I'm making for dinner, and what I'm doing for exercise. I also include any appointments I have scheduled. That's it. It takes me less than two minutes, but it gives me focus and direction for my entire day. More importantly, it helps me filter out the tasks and commitments that threaten to steal time away from my larger goals.

Do you have a system for setting and keeping your goals?

Action Step: Even if you are doing this Bible study in the middle of the year, it's not too late or too early to set some big goals for the remainder of the year. What are some things you would like to accomplish this year? Write them here.

In your walk with God:

_____

_____

In your ministry:

_____

_____

In your job:

_____

_____

In your relationships:

_____

_____

In your health:

_____

_____

In your finances:

_____

_____

From the things you've written, pick the one that means the most to you. Set a mini-monthly goal for that one thing:

_____

_____

Now, write one thing you will do tomorrow to support that mini goal:

_____

_____

9. Mind your own business.

I do not believe our hearts were designed to carry the amount of personal information social media feeds us. (Oh no. I feel another social media rant coming on!)

It used to be that relationships naturally began and ended. We'd grow up, graduate from school, move houses, relocate, and change jobs. We'd say goodbye to old neighbors, classmates, and co-workers, making room in our lives for new neighbors, classmates, and co-workers. Within those relationships, only a handful of them transcended distance and time. (Those friends are awesome, by the way. If you have transcendent friends, stop and thank God for them right now.) Unless someone lived in the same house with us, we rarely knew intimate details of their day-to-day lives.

Now, we have constant contact with every person we've ever known since we were born. We meet someone new in the church lobby and have a "friend request" waiting for us by lunchtime. The next day, and every day following, we know when our new friend goes on vacation, what articles they find interesting, what instrument their child plays, and who they voted for in the last election.

The relationships never end. Which sounds sweet, until you consider the amount of time and energy it takes to keep up with all these people. How can we make room in our schedule (or our hearts!) for new relationships when minutia from the lives of every person we have ever known (and some we don't!) clutters our news feed?

Additionally, we now have the ability to *emote and opine* about their vacations, their favorite articles, their children, and their political affiliations. We shouldn't even know these things, yet we do—plus, we know *what everyone else thinks about them.*

Never before in the history of the world do we have opportunity to be in everyone's business like we do today.

It's all too much.

A few years ago, while my 4-year-old daughter was playing in the bathtub, I was in the middle of a Facebook debate over religion with a girl who attended my church when I was 18-years-old. I wouldn't even call this girl a friend. I hardly knew her, even then. I had not seen her in 35 years. She currently lives in another state. If I saw her in person today I doubt we would recognize each other. Yet, here I was, in a heated theological debate, while my preschool daughter played alone in the bathtub next to me.

As my daughter splashed and played, my heart rate continued to rise over stupid things this girl was saying—things that held no place in my hierarchy of priorities. I was literally typing with one hand as I was washing my daughter's back with the other.

That's when I recognized the absurdity of the situation and of social media in general.

That night, I deactivated my Facebook account in an attempt to step back and assess the role social media would play in my life.

The deactivation lasted several weeks. Before I reactivated my account, I redefined my relationship with social media. I "un-friended" people who are not my friends in real life. I blocked highly opinionated and negative people from seeing my posts. I hid almost everyone from my feed—forcing me to type the names of my actual friends and family into the search engine when I want to see an update.

If you find yourself constantly pulled into social media drama, getting upset over political rants, or devoting massive amounts of emotional energy worrying about things you shouldn't even know, then perhaps it's time to mind your own business. Turn to your actual priorities and busy yourself there. Take a social media break. Hide people from your feed. Guard your heart against information that diverts your attention away from your highest priorities.

In your Bible, look up 1 Thessalonians 4:11-12 and fill in the blanks below:

"and to make it your ambition to lead a _____ _____: You should_____ _____ _____ and to work with your hands, just as we told you, so that your daily life may win the _____ _____ _____ and so that you will not be dependent on anybody."

Action Step: Think about your social media accounts. How do you feel when you are on social media? Circle all the words that apply, even if they are conflicting:

happy   fulfilled   informed   anxious   worried

connected   empty   lazy   productive   content   inspired

overwhelmed   ugly   depressed   beautiful   unproductive

balanced   discontent   lonely   jealous   sad   energized

222| FINDING YOUR BALANCE

Describe your relationship with social media here: (For example, are you indifferent to it? Are you addicted to it? Are you something in between?)

If you are not active on social media, what other relationships lead you to know more about people than you should? Do you have a friend who uses you as a sounding board for gossip? Does your work break room become a breeding ground for office gossip? Does your mom disclose details about your siblings, their finances, their marriage problems, and their kids?

If knowing too much about other people is contributing to your busyness, what will you do about it? What can you do today to guard your heart?

---

10. Make rest a priority. What? Who has time to rest when we are already so busy? It may sound counterintuitive, but it's not. Rest was God's idea. He modeled rest for us from day one...I mean, *Day Seven*:

Read Genesis 2:2-3.

What is God doing in this passage?

Rest comes in many forms. In order to undo the busyness that holds you in bondage, I recommend you prioritize nightly, weekly, and annual rest.

Nightly

Nightly rest is integral to your health, both physically and mentally. It is only during a good night's sleep that vital brain functions take place, such as, the natural production and release of human growth hormone (instrumental in metabolizing fat) and the transferring of information from short-term memory to long-term memory.

In your Bible, look up Mark 6:31. Paraphrase it here:

_____

_____

_____

Weekly

In the Old Testament, God considered weekly rest so important, He actually drafted it into the Law.

Read Leviticus 23:3 in your Bible, then fill in the blanks.

"There are six days when you may work, but the seventh day is a day of _____ _____, a day of sacred assembly. You are _____ _____ _____ _____ _____; wherever you live, it is a sabbath to the _____."

While Christians are under a New Covenant and no longer bound by Old Testament law, prioritizing weekly rest from work still makes good sense. Depending upon your job, this either sounds incredible or impossible. Or both. I get it. For a long time, I felt frustrated with my attempts at taking a Sabbath. As a stay-at-home/work-from-home mom with a busy family of five, it felt like punishment whenever I attempted to take a break, even for one day. My kids still needed to eat. The laundry spawned offspring. The dirty dishes refused to wash themselves, no matter how desperately I begged them to do so. How could I possibly pull this off?

Then I read about The Day of Preparation, which was the day before the Sabbath:

In your Bible, read Exodus 16:23 and 29.

On the sixth day, God commanded them to make enough food for two days. Duh! Why didn't I think of this? This changed everything for me! Now, if I intend to rest from cooking, I make sure I've prepared enough food for two days, or I arrange for us to eat out. If I am going to skip a laundry day, I do an extra load or two the day before. If I'm going to skip a cleaning day, I'll set out paper plates and plastic wear. I may even do a little extra tidying up so I can truly relax.

Annually

Consider taking at least a week (or two, or more!) annually for vacation and rest from all work. It's like hitting a reset button on your computer. Speaking of computers, consider leaving yours at home while vacationing.

Taking these intentional breaks from the hurry and busyness of life forces us to slow down and recharge. It also confirms, once and for all, that the world will not, in fact, fall off its axis if we step off to rest.

Action Steps: For the next week, make it a top priority to get at least eight hours of sleep every night. Notice how much better you feel at the end of the week. Write down whatever obstacles you foresee in getting a good night's sleep. What can you do to overcome them?

What day of the week works best for a weekly Sabbath? It doesn't have to be Sunday. Maybe it's Tuesday…

What are some things you can do ahead of time to prepare for your Sabbath day?

Do you have a vacation planned this year? Get one on the calendar. Don't worry now about where or how much it will cost. Just designate a week in the next 12 months to step away from work and spend time with your loved ones.

It's Time to Start Bailing

If you are living a busy, hurried life, you cannot sustain this pace for the long-term. You must remove some things from your schedule, or you'll sink. Hopefully, as you moved through this lesson and this Bible study, you eliminated unnecessary commitments, simplified something, and took control of your social media usage. Congratulations! This is a great start. I bet you feel better already.

If you are crazy-busy—if your little boat is sinking and small changes are not enough—you may need a more radical approach. You may need to tip your sinking boat over and dump all the water out entirely. Don't be afraid to do this. Balance is too important to live in a constantly hurried, hectic state. Take the hiatus. Deactivate the social media accounts. Find your replacement for the volunteer committee. Cancel the piano lessons. Tell your boss you can no longer work overtime. Find a new job. Do whatever you need to do to ruthlessly eliminate hurry from your life. Your balance depends on it.

Before we conclude this final lesson, take a minute to record your three take-aways

1. _____

2. _____

3. _____

Let's pray:

Lord,

I know that time is of the essence. There is no time to waste, so I will not complicate my life unnecessarily. I will keep it simple—in marriage, grief, joy. Even in ordinary things—my daily routines. I will deal as sparingly as possible with the things the world thrusts on me. The world as I see it is on its way out.

For godliness with contentment is great gain. I brought nothing into the world, and I will take nothing out of it. If I have food and clothing, I will be content with that. Keep falsehood and lies far from me; give me neither poverty nor riches, but give me only my daily bread.

I will be very careful how I live—not as unwise but as wise, making the most of every opportunity because the days are evil.

Help me know and recognize the gifts You have given me. Show me how to use them for the common good in the Body of Christ and to say no to things I am not equipped by You to do. Help me recognize the seasons, knowing there is a time for everything.

Help me prioritize rest. Help me get a good night's sleep every night. Help me to set aside time every week to stop my regular work and seek You. You are my rest.

I will make it my ambition to lead a quiet life, to mind my own business and work with my hands, so that my daily life may win the respect of outsiders.

I know you simply want me to entrust my time to You, knowing that when I use it to serve others and build Your kingdom, you promise to reward me with treasures in heaven.

In Jesus' name.

Amen.

Conclusion

Well girls, we made it. If you were with me in person, we'd end with a special celebration, most certainly involving food. And confetti.

Over the course of our journey together, we've deconstructed faulty images of balance (unicorns included) and in their place, created a new, viable goal based entirely on God's word.

We've boasted about our weaknesses so that Christ's power will rest upon us.

We've reordered our priorities and our calendars.

We've demolished barriers, watched them crumble at our feet, and confidently stepped over each and every one.

We've declared God's word over our hearts and minds and asked Him to permeate every meaningful area of our lives.

We've learned afresh how to love God and love people.

If you worked through this Bible study at the rate of one lesson per week, you and I have spent nearly three months together. I don't know about you, but whenever I finish a Bible study of this length, I always feel a little lost. After months of digging deeply into God's word with guidance and purpose, suddenly, I'm at the end and I'm like, *What do I do now?*

My hope for you is that you continue in the direction you have been walking. I hope you continue chipping away at the balance barriers most obstructive to you. As seasons change, I hope you continue to identify your priorities and pursue them with focus and determination.

Balance is ever-changing because *you* are ever-changing. That means you may need reminders from time to time to help you stay on course. Obviously, you can always go back and review what you've learned here. (I've been known to rework Bible studies multiple times.) You may even want to teach this Bible study to someone else. (I'd be so stinking proud of you if you did this).

For ongoing support and encouragement, you can visit me on my blog where I have written hundreds of posts on balance (www.thescooponbalance.com). I'd love to connect with you there and hear how this Bible study has helped you and what you plan to do next.

Whatever you do from here, I hope you find *peace and freedom in Christ*, knowing that balance is well within your reach.

Love,

Sandy

Acknowledgments

Jon: Thank you for holding down the fort and cheering me on while I hid out in the writing cave. Your love and encouragement makes me brave. This will be a great year for us; I'm sure of it.

Rebekah: Thank you for being patient with me as I trudged through the process of learning to balance my priorities—the majority of which occurred during your lifetime (sorry). You have grown into an outstanding young adult in spite of my faulty parenting. You are truly one of the funniest people I know (and you know, coming from me, that is the highest compliment I could possibly give). Whatever path you choose, you'll crush it. I'm so incredibly proud of you.

Elijah: Thank you for always being impressed whenever I gave you my updated word count. Your enthusiasm for life and writing inspires me. If God lined up all the boys in the whole world and told me I could pick one, I'd pick you.

Elliana: Thank you for always asking, "How's the Bible study going?" And also, for singing with me in the kitchen and in the car. I don't know how our family ever survived without you. You are joy personified.

Ana: Thank you for being my OLBFF for the last decade—your friendship means the world to me. Also, thank you for making me a stronger writer and for working your hilarious reactions all throughout your corrections. You make the revision process almost enjoyable.

James: Thank you for telling me at the age of 18 that I could teach a Bible study.

Cynthia: Thank you for starting me on my pathway to freedom.

Tim: Thank you for inspiring me to be a better communicator and for teaching me how to truly study the Bible. When I asked for a recommendation for a good Bible commentary, you showed me a literal wall full of your favorites. Thank you also for entrusting me with the women of New Life Church, for always believing in everything I do, and constantly encouraging me to continue writing.

Every group of women who has gathered either in person or on the Internet to listen to me teach some version of this study: Thank you for your comments, feedback, and input. You have helped shaped this study into something relevant.

Jesus Christ: Thank you for modeling a perfectly balanced life.

About the Author

Sandy Cooper is the Leader of Women's Ministry at New Life Church in Louisville, Kentucky, a Bible study teacher for the last 30 years, and author of her personal blog, *The Scoop on Balance.* (www.thescooponbalance.com)

Her greatest accomplishments include surviving the death of her 9-month-old son (Noah), winning her daily battle against clinical depression, and finding a laundry system that actually works (The search for which may or may not have contributed to the depression).

She loves exercise, cooking, and being home, where she lives with Jon (her husband of 24 years) and her three living children: Rebekah (18), Elijah (16) and Elliana (10).

End Notes

Lesson One

[1] Erin Loechner (2016) *Chasing Slow: Courage to Journey Off the Beaten Path.* Grand Rapids, MI: Zondervan.

Lesson Three

[2] Ortberg, John (2007) *When the Game is Over It All Goes Back in the Box.* Grand Rapids, MI: Zondervan.

[3] Ibid.

[4] Francis Chan and Lisa Chan (2014) *You and Me Forever: Marriage in Light of Eternity.* San Francisco, CA: Claire Love Publishing.

[5] *Propaganda to Mobilize Women for World War II*, Susan Mathis, http://www.socialstudies.org/sites/default/files/publications/se/5802/580210.html

[6] Cambridge Bible for School and Colleges, via Bible Gateway.com

[7] Sally Clarkson and Nathan Clarkson (2016) *Different: The Story of an Outside-the-Box Kid and the Mom Who Loved Him.* Carol Stream, IL: Tyndale Momentum.

Lesson Four

[8] Hugh Prather (1970) *Notes to Myself: My Struggle to Become a Person.* New York, NY: Bantam Books.

[9] York University. (2004, June 14). Perfectionism Can Lead To Imperfect Health: High Achievers More Prone To Emotional, Physical And Relationship Problems. *ScienceDaily.* Retrieved February 18, 2017 from www.sciencedaily.com/releases/2004/06/040614074620.htm

[10] ibid.

[11] https://www.psychologytoday.com/blog/dont-delay/200804/what-flavor-perfectionist-are-you-it-matters

[12] http://www.drmargaretjordan.com/perfectionism/

Lesson Five

[13] Niequist, Shauna (2016) *Present Over Perfect: Leaving Behind Frantic for a Simpler, More Soulful Way of Living*. Grand Rapids, MI: Zondervan, p. 197.

[14] The best resource I have read related to this process is the book *Boundaries: When to Say Yes, When to Say No—to Take Control of Your Life*, by Dr. Henry Cloud and Dr. John Townsend. Consider reading this book as supplemental material to this Bible study.

Lesson Six

[15] This quote is most commonly attributed to Theodore Roosevelt or Christian author Dwight Edwards.

Lesson Seven

[16] Hatmaker, Jen (2015) *For the Love: Fighting for Grace in a World of Impossible Standards*. Nashville, TN: Nelson Books, p. 5.

[17] Terkeurst, Lysa (2010) *Made to Crave: Satisfying Your Deepest Desire With God, Not Food*. Grand Rapids, MI: Zondervan, p. 184.

[18] Actual quotes from my children, Rebekah and Elijah Cooper

Lesson Eight

[19] This quote is all over Pinterest with no source referenced. After an Internet search, I found a paper by this name written by Sally Rose published in *The British Journal of Psychotherapy Integration*. I have no idea if this is the original author of the quote, but it is the most credible source I could locate, so she shall receive the credit.

[20] http://drlescarter.com/2015/06/11/are-you-a-people-pleaser/

Lesson Nine

[21] Cloud, Henry and Townsend, John (1992) *Boundaries: When to Say Yes, How to Say No to Take Control of Your Life*. Grand Rapids, MI: Zondervan, p. 47.

Lesson Ten

[22] Twitter, October 20, 2009.

[23] http://www.christianitytoday.com/pastors/1998/fall/8l4028.html

[24] http://www.christianitytoday.com/pastors/1998/fall/8l4028.html

[25] http://www.cnn.com/2001/CAREER/trends/08/05/multitasking.fo

cus/index.html

[26] http://www.mayoclinic.org/healthy-lifestyle/stress-management/in-depth/stress-symptoms/art-20050987

[27] http://www.socialmediatoday.com/marketing/how-much-time-do-people-spend-social-media-infographic

[28] http://www.networkworld.com/article/3092446/smartphones/we-touch-our-phones-2617-times-a-day-says-study.html

Lesson Eleven

[29] McKeown, Greg, (2014) *Essentialism: The Disciplined Pursuit of Less.* New York, NY: Crown Publishing, pg 221.

[30] If you have never taken a spiritual gifting test, I highly suggest you do so. Several free versions exist on line, such as the one found here: https://spiritualgiftstest.com/spiritual-gifts-test-adult-version/
Two resources that helped me pinpoint my spiritual gifts and strengths and also showed me how to use them in the Church are Max Lucado's book *Cure for the Common Life* and Rick Warren's book, *The Purpose-Driven Life*.

Made in the USA
Columbia, SC
18 August 2024